Hooked on Rugs

Outstanding Contemporary Designs

Jessie A. Turbayne

Schiffer Publishing Ltd

4880 Lower Valley Road, Atglen, PA 19310 USA

Dedication

To the Girls

Other Schiffer Books by Jessie A. Turbayne
The Big Book of Hooked Rugs: 1950-1980s
The Complete Guide to Collecting Hooked Rugs: Unrolling the Secrets
The Hooker's Art: Evolving Designs in Hooked Rugs
Hooked Rug Treasury
Hooked Rugs: History and the Continuing Tradition

Other Schiffer Books on Related Subjects
Hooked Rugs Today, by Amy Oxford
Punch Needle Rug Hooking: Techniques and Designs, by Amy Oxford

---

Library of Congress Control Number: 2006922996

Designed by "Sue"
Type set in Zapf Humanist Demi BT/Novarese Bk BT

ISBN: 0-7643-2502-7
Printed in China

Published by Schiffer Publishing Ltd.
4880 Lower Valley Road
Atglen, PA 19310
Phone: (610) 593-1777; Fax: (610) 593-2002
E-mail: Info@schifferbooks.com

For the largest selection of fine reference books on this and related subjects, please visit our web site at
www.schifferbooks.com
We are always looking for people to write books on new and related subjects. If you have an idea for a book please contact us at the above address.

This book may be purchased from the publisher.
Include $3.95 for shipping.
Please try your bookstore first.
You may write for a free catalog.

In Europe, Schiffer books are distributed by
Bushwood Books
6 Marksbury Ave.
Kew Gardens
Surrey TW9 4JF England
Phone: 44 (0) 20 8392-8585; Fax: 44 (0) 20 8392-9876
E-mail: info@bushwoodbooks.co.uk
Website: www.bushwoodbooks.co.uk
Free postage in the U.K., Europe; air mail at cost.

Contents

Acknowledgments

I wish to extend my sincere gratitude to those who contributed to the making of this book:

A very special word of thanks to my editor, Donna Baker, and Schiffer Publishing Ltd.

Heartfelt appreciation to:

All the rug hooking artists who so kindly shared their work and enthusiasm.

Michael, for always being there.

Jamie, for starting all of this.

Judi Yasi, my New England Technical Editor and Advisor, for always being patient with those of us who should never venture into the world of modern technology. Thank you for your insight, input, and much needed humor.

Marge Mello, who has traveled near and far with me in search of hooked rugs and has never said no when I asked. We all need a friend like you. Book the flight for Bhutan!

Kind acknowledgements to: Susan Andreson; The Cranberry Hookers Guild; Nancy Baker; Rebecca Erb; Linda Euse; John Flournoy; Chris Gooding; The Green Mountain Guild; Rae Reynolds Harrell; Anna King; Linda Litter; June Mikoryak; Scott Morrison, SDS Computers; Mary Lee O'Connor; Rob Petta and Molly Cox; Linda Rapasky; June Robbs; Annie Spring; The Tiger Ladies; C. Allan Turbayne; Justina Rae Two Eagle and Jan Winter.

For hooked pieces not photographed by me, kind acknowledgements to:

Those who provided me with photographs, slides, and digital images of their work.

Photographers: J.J. Hamer for Suzanne S. Hamer; Tim Ayers for Anna King; Ray Llanas for Joyce Krueger; and Michael Reynolds, Michael Reynolds Photography, Plymouth, Michigan, for June Mikoryak and her students.

Introduction

So you think no one hand-hooks rugs anymore? That the craft went out with whale oil lamps and horse and buggies? Well,...think again my friend. Tens of thousands of women, men, and children are hooking rugs just as they did in the mid-1800s. What has changed is the *reason* they hook. Gone are the days when thrifty individuals ripped up rags and worn out clothing to create warm floor coverings for drafty homes. Today's rug makers hook to express their creativity. They hook for pleasure, enjoying the simple stress-relieving process of pulling strips of woolen fabric (or yarn) through a loosely woven foundation. The results are tactilely and aesthetically pleasing—works of art that complement floors, walls, and so much more.

Unlike their rug making ancestors, modern fiber artists have access to a wide variety of hooking supplies. Whether working from a pre-printed pattern or creating their own design, artists can use hooking foundations (burlap, linen, monk's cloth, etc.) that are woven for durability and strength, insuring long life. Hooking frames, used to keep foundations taut while the rug is worked, are available in numerous stationary and portable models. Woolen fabric, used as is or hand-dyed in a rainbow of shades, can be ripped, cut by hand, or cut by using a hand-cranked or electric cutter. Many of these cutters feature multiple interchangeable heads capable of slicing strips of woolen fabric as thin as 2/32" wide. Also available are rug hooking scissors with specially angled blades to assure ease and neatness when sculpting hooked loops or snipping stray ends. And, of course, there is a hook for every hand: simple and straightforward or ornate and silver-plated.

Although some choose to work alone, rug hooking has gone uptown and become a social activity, bringing together interested artists from all walks of life. There are rug hooking camps, workshops, luxurious hooking getaways, weekly classes, exhibits, shows, and gala rug hooking events. Rug hookers love to socialize with other rug hookers.

"Flutter By Fantasy." Designed by Jane McGown Flynn. House of Price / Charco pattern. Hooked by Suzanne S. Hamer. Illinois. 1996. 16.5" x 27". *Courtesy of Suzanne S. Hamer.*

When the word was out that I was planning to do a new book featuring contemporary hooked rugs—i.e., those ten years or younger—the response from rugs hookers across the United States, Canada, and beyond was overwhelming. Hooking artists not only submitted images for consideration, they showed up in droves with armloads of rugs when photo shoots were announced. I soon realized I had enough material for not one but two books. I am sure that after viewing *Hooked on Rugs: Outstanding Contemporary Designs*, you will agree that rug hooking is alive, well, and thriving.

Note: Hooked rug measurements have been rounded to the nearest half inch. All rugs are hooked on burlap, rug hooking linen, monk's cloth, cotton warp, or other foundations using cut strips of woolen fabric unless noted. In some cases of special interest, the hooking materials have been listed. Using information supplied by rug owners as well as my own research, all efforts have been made to properly identify rug hookers, titles of their work, dates of completion, dimensions, and names of patterns and pattern makers. The author claims no responsibility for any misidentification. All hooked pieces adapted from the work of other artists were done so with permission. Permission was obtained by the hooking artist and not the author. The author claims no responsibility for any copyright infringements.

The tools of the trade: as is and hand-dyed woolen fabrics, an assortment of hooks, rug hooking scissors, and cutter.

"Rosalita." Designed and hooked by Jule Marie Smith. New York. 2004. 15" x 15". *Courtesy of Jule Marie Smith.*

"Wild Cherries." Lib Callaway pattern / Hook Nook. Hooked by Kathie Barbour. New Hampshire. 2000. 33" x 42". *Courtesy of Kathie Barbour.*

Rug makers cut the woolen fabric they hook with into a wide variety of widths. The Townsend Cutter makes that job a cinch. *Courtesy of the Townsend Industries Inc.*

For ease and comfort while hooking, rug makers stretch their rug's foundation across specially designed frames. The Townsend "Orbiter" frame offers all that any rug hooker could want. *Courtesy of the Townsend Industries Inc.*

Work In Progress

When it comes to understanding how a rug is hooked, it is not only interesting but helpful to see a work in progress.

A work in progress. Depicted is the rug's foundation with a hand-drawn pattern and partially hooked design. "Kathe's Platter." Adapted from an antique flow blue platter. Designed and hooked by Beth Kempf. Connecticut. 2005. Finished size 36" x 28". *Courtesy of Beth Kempf.*

Detail of a yet to be completed "Tin Peddler." Charlotte Stratton / Yankee Peddler pattern. Hooked by Rosalie Lent. Maine. 2005. *Courtesy of Rosalie Lent.*

"Pansies for Thoughts" well underway. Heirloom Rug pattern. Hooked by Shirley Teasdale. Maine. 2005. Finished size 27" x 38". *Courtesy of Shirley Teasdale.*

The Hookers' World of Geometric Designs

Geometric designs are ageless and attract a wide and varied audience. Whether your home features simple country antiques or high-end ultra modern furniture, there is a geometric-style hooked rug to coordinate with any décor and to suit every need and taste.

Bold, graphic, and pleasing to the eye. "Parcheesi Board" was "inspired by antique game boards and the dream of family members playing games under my great-grandmother's Tiffany lamp." Designed and hooked by Karen Cooper. New Hampshire. 2004. 25" x 25". *Courtesy of Karen Cooper.*

Everyday objects are transformed into a kaleidoscope image. "I needed a pattern for a geometrics class I was scheduled to take and saw the beautiful ad for the Pozzi Windows. That, I decided, would be my project." "Window Frames." Adapted with permission from an ad by JELD-WEN® Pozzi Custom Collection Wood Windows, as shown in *Southern Living Magazine* 2003. Hooked by Valerie A. Johnston. North Carolina. 2004. 33" x 33". *Courtesy of Valerie A. Johnston and JELD-WEN® Pozzi Custom Collection Wood Windows.*

Intended to be much smaller, "Geometric Garden" just grew and grew. Designed and hooked by Christi Winter. California. 2001. 72" x 59". *Courtesy of Christi Winter.*

Alternating concentric "Circles and Squares" line up. Adapted from a quilt pattern. Polly Reinhart. Pennysylvania. 2001. 22" x 27". *Courtesy of Polly Reinhart.*

"I forgot to bring my rug to class one week and my teacher, Jacqueline Hansen, suggested I go into the back room, quit whining, and draw some circles." Yankee ingenuity at its best. "Circles." Designed and hooked by Jeni Nunnally. Maine. 2004. 24" x 32". *Courtesy of Jeni Nunnally.*

"6 Red Circles" bring vibrant color to a tradition quilt pattern. Designed and hooked by Polly Reinhart. Pennsylvania. 2003. 23.5" x 31". *Courtesy of Polly Reinhart.*

Images of Ferris wheels and circus wagon wheels were in her thoughts when Thelma Kirkhoff hooked twenty-three circles. "Pinwheels and Circles." Designed and hooked by Thelma P. Kirkhoff. Pennsylvania. 2004. 40" x 24". *Courtesy of Thelma P. Kirkhoff.*

Quartered circles in warm, earthy tones are contained by concentric borders. Adapted from a quilt pattern. "Quarter Circles." Designed and hooked by Polly Reinhart. Pennsylvania. 2004. 22" x 26". *Courtesy of Polly Reinhart.*

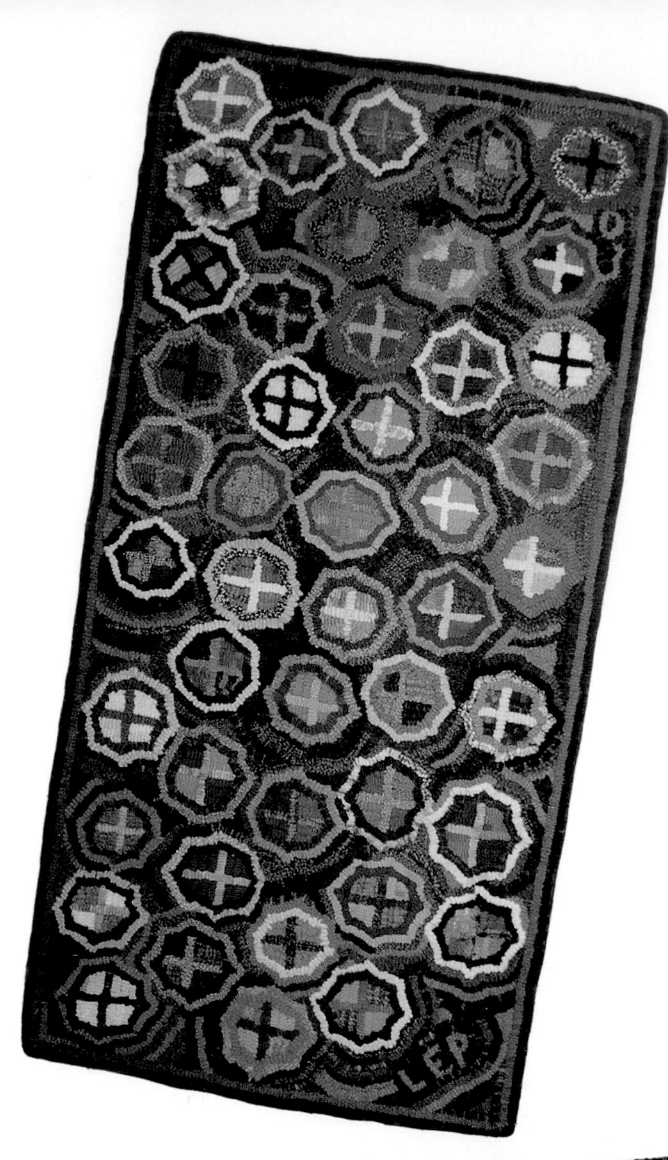

Irregularly shaped and quartered "Circles" dance on a variegated field. Barbara Brown pattern. Hooked by Laura Phinney. Maine. 2003. 47" x 23". *Courtesy of Laura Phinney.*

Three rows of concentric hexagons are reminiscent of a traditional quilt pattern. Designed by Richard O'Connor. Hooked by Kathy O'Connor. Pennsylvania. 2003. 35" x 16". *Courtesy of Kathy O'Connor.*

Woolen fabric leftovers from other projects were used to fashion this angular collage. "Rectangles and Squares." Adapted from a rug belonging to Evelyn Lawrence. Hooked by Thelma P. Kirkhoff. Pennsylvania. 2004. 29" x 40". *Courtesy of Thelma P. Kirkhoff.*

Pearl Stoudt came to hooking late in life. At age seventy-five, she signed up for a five-week course and has been hooking ever since. Now in her early eighties, she finds that making rugs gets her up every morning and lets her feel creative. "Basket Weave." Designed and hooked by Pearl Stoudt. Pennsylvania. 2002. 45" x 54". *Courtesy of Pearl Stoudt.*

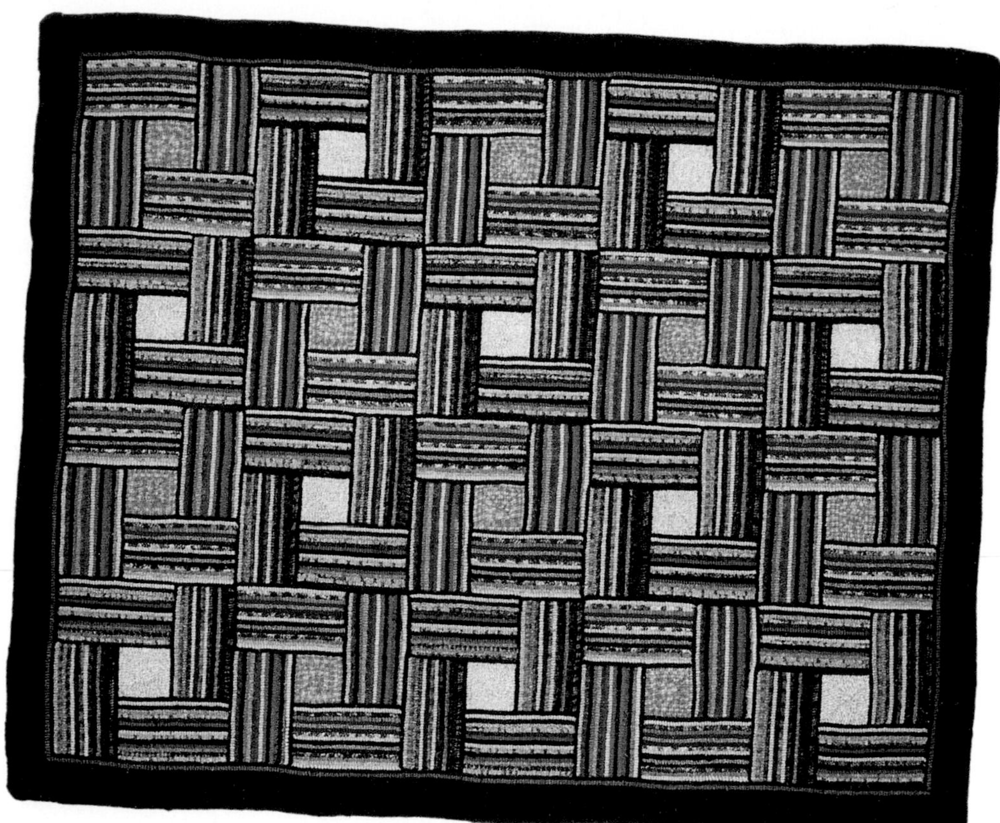

Hooked stripes form woven bands. "Hit or Miss." Designed and hooked by Pearl Stoudt. Pennsylvania. 2000. 50" x 39". *Courtesy of Pearl Stoudt.*

"Tumbling Blocks." "Each cube has a dark, medium, and light surface, placed with no apparent order. The effect is to keep the eye moving and the combination of textured wool and plain wool, adds visual interest." "Traditional." Designed by Jane McGown Flynn. House of Price / Charco pattern. Hooked by Susan Higgins. California. 1997. 18" x 30". *Courtesy of Susan Higgins.*

Clamshells galore in a limited palette. "Shell Geometric." Designed by Jane McGown Flynn. House of Price / Charco pattern. Hooked by Cyndee S. Brandt. Texas. 2004. 39.5" x 22". *Courtesy of Cyndee S. Brandt.*

Another interpretation of the traditional clamshell pattern. "Shell Geometric." Designed by Jane McGown Flynn. House of Price / Charco pattern. Hooked by Tricia Travis. Texas. 2003. 39.5" x 22". *Courtesy of Tricia Travis.*

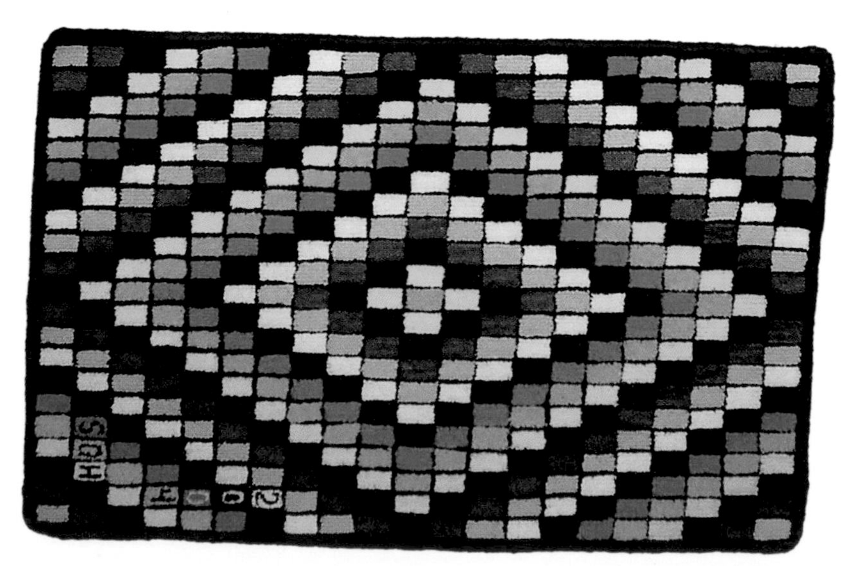

Rug hookers love quilt patterns and Sue Hammond is no exception. The inspiration for "Blue and Gold Geometric" was an Amish quilt. Squares were replaced by rectangles. Designed and hooked by Sue Hammond. New Hampshire. 2004. 23" x 35". *Courtesy of Sue Hammond.*

A trio of sunflowers, complete with raised and sculptured ladybugs, rests upon a geometric field. "Inch Mat with Sunflowers." Designed and hooked by Lois Egenes. Iowa. 2001. 26" x 46". *Courtesy of Lois Egenes.*

Hooking artist Liz Alpert Fay puts a contemporary spin on an old quilt pattern. The turquoise frame was hooked then embroidered with strips of hooking wool. Button embellishments and yarn embroidery decorate the outer black woolen fabric border. "Compass Variation." Designed and hooked by Liz Alpert Fay. Connecticut. 2004. 78" x 48". *Courtesy of Liz Alpert Fay.*

Details of "Compass Variation." *Courtesy of Liz Alpert Fay.*

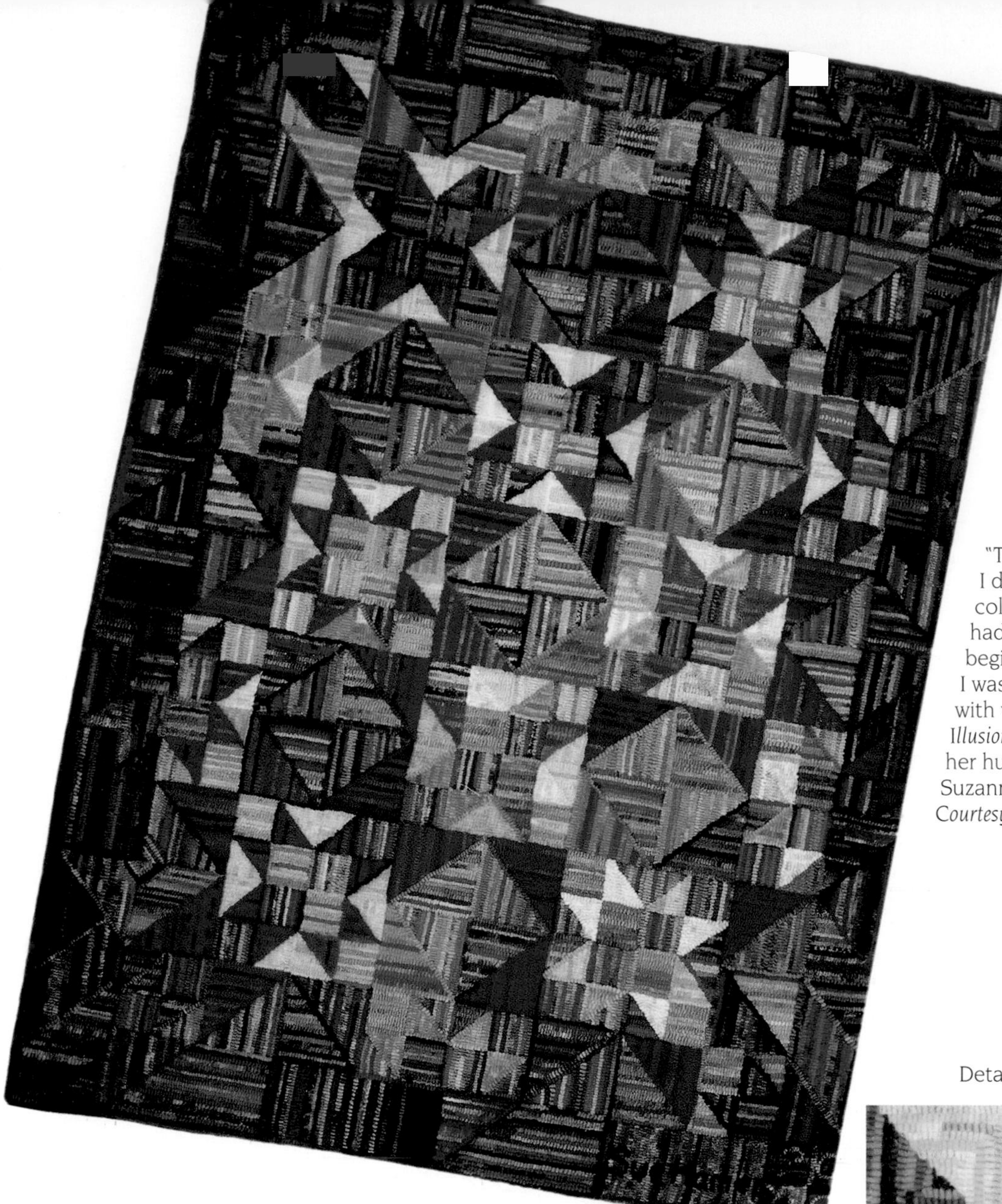

"The design for this rug was instantaneous. I did one drawing and one color plan. The colors are brighter and livelier than any I had done before. The border reflects the beginning of my life going in a new direction. I was 'Transformed.'" In addition to hooking with woolen fabric, the artist used strips of *Illusion* metallic fiber and small bits of silk from her husband's ties. Designed and hooked by Suzanne S. Hamer. Illinois. 2000. 42" x 30". *Courtesy of Suzanne S. Hamer.*

Detail of "Color Play." *Courtesy of Sharon Saknit.*

"Color Play." "I designed this rug so that the 'V's of color following the color wheel would have inverted 'V's of light and dark superimposed on them." Designed and hooked by Sharon Saknit. California. 2004. 30" x 44.5". *Courtesy of Sharon Saknit.*

The pattern for "Twisted Ribbons" creates an optical illusion. Adapted from an old quilt pattern. Hooked by Judith Dallegret. Montreal, Canada. 2003. 30" x 48". *Courtesy of Judith Dallegret.*

Three versions of the same pattern. "Playing with Color." Designed and hooked by Suzanne S. Hamer. Illinois. 2003. Each piece 17.5" x 13.5". *Courtesy of Suzanne S. Hamer.*

A multitude of diamond patterns hooked in "Relative Values." Designed and hooked by Suzanne S. Hamer. Illinois. 2004. 37" x 23". *Courtesy of Suzanne S. Hamer.*

Triangles become squares. Light plays against dark. "Fiber Optics." Designed and hooked by Suzanne S. Hamer. Illinois. 1997. 36" x 24". *Courtesy of* Suzanne S. Hamer.

"Stained Glass Triangles" reminds one of light coming through a window. Designed and hooked by Polly Reinhart. Pennsylvania. 2003. 20" x 27". *Courtesy of Polly Reinhart.*

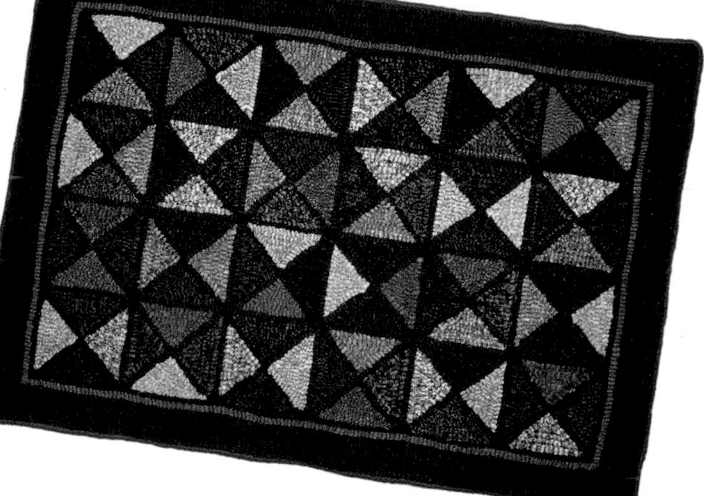

"This rug was hooked for my then teenage son. I wanted to capture the simplicity of a relatively traditional geometric design of circles and intersecting lines, choosing a red, tan, and black palette. But I also wanted the piece to reflect my son's free spirit. So, I added squares of bright color at each intersection and decided that a few of these should occasionally 'explode' into asymmetrical stars. I wanted to break the perfection of the pattern, and, after much thought, decided that the stars should break into the border of the rug." "Geometric." Designed by Pearl McGown. W. Cushing and Company pattern. Hooked by Susan Higgins. California. 1997. 24" x 33". *Courtesy of Susan Higgins.*

Nine diamonds dance on a dark field. Colorful stripes frame the pattern. "Color Study One." Designed and hooked by Suzanne S. Hamer. Illinois. 1997. 24" x 24". *Courtesy of Suzanne S. Hamer.*

"The circles represent the fullness of my life and many of the worlds that have brought me such satisfaction and joy. The colors I used included the entire color wheel." "My Many Worlds—Color Study Two." Designed and hooked by Suzanne S. Hamer. Illinois. 2003. 31" x 31". *Courtesy of Suzanne S. Hamer.*

A central red cross is held within fanciful borders. "Border Madness." Designed and hooked by Carol Morris Petillo. Maine. 2004. 31" x 31". *Courtesy of Carol Morris Petillo.*

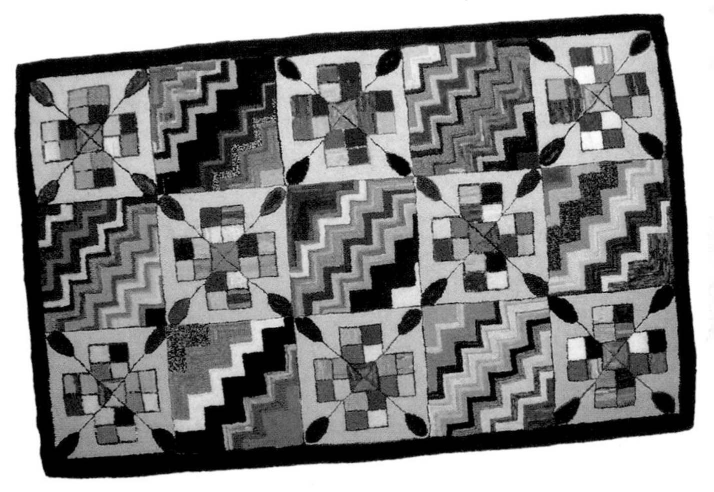

Bright and colorful, the "Crossed Paddles" pattern is an old favorite among rug hookers. Heirloom Rug pattern. Hooked by Judy Howarth. Maine. 2002. 29" x 42". *Courtesy of Judy Howarth.*

Five stars hooked with love for grandson, Michael Boisseau. "Mike's Stars." Designed and hooked by Betsy Gerakaris. Connecticut. 2001. 24" x 33". *Courtesy of Betsy Gerakaris.*

"Symmetry." "I played with only three colors and a couple of values. My goal was to try for a harmonious rug. Special attention was paid to the direction of hooking to enhance the texture and also to the dyeing for the border and yarn used to whip stitch the outer edge." "Symmetry." Designed by Jane McGown Flynn. House of Price / Charco pattern. Hooked by Tony Latham. Quebec, Canada. 2004. 26" x 45". *Courtesy of Tony Latham.*

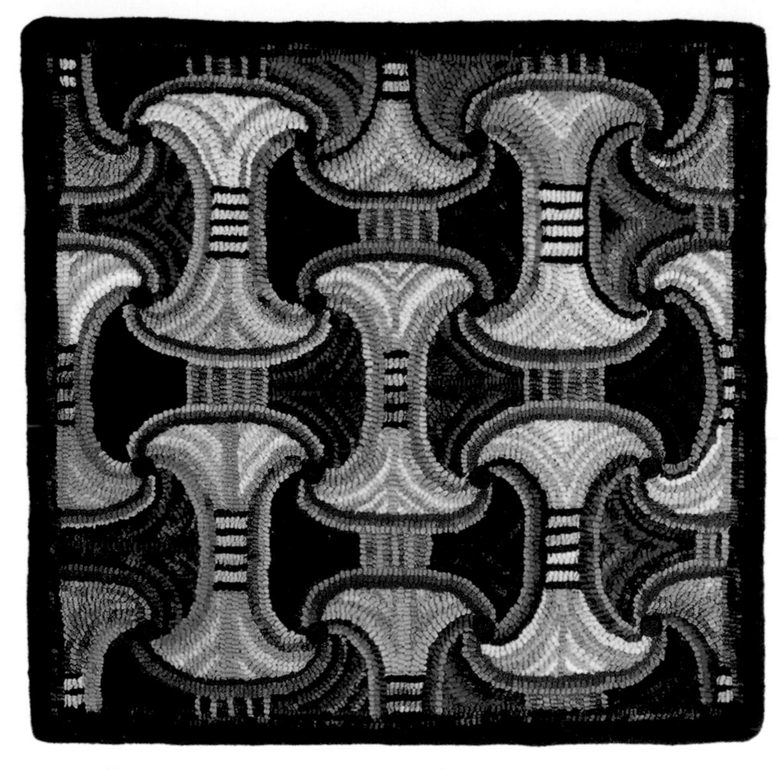

A smaller version of the aforementioned "Symmetry" pattern. Sixteen small buttons were added to the interlocking edges of the spool-like shapes. Designed by Jane McGown Flynn. House of Price / Charo pattern. Hooked by Suzanne S. Hamer. Illinois. 2004. 17" x 17". *Courtesy of Suzanne S. Hamer.*

Diamonds within a diamond. "Split Geometric." Designed and hooked by Suzanne S. Hamer. Illinois. 2004. 22" x 22". *Courtesy of Suzanne S. Hamer.*

Quilt square patterns are transformed into hooked mats. "Quilts to Rugs." Designed and hooked by Suzanne S. Hamer. Illinois. 2004. Each piece 8" x 8". *Courtesy of Suzanne S. Hamer.*

A hooked quilt pattern is fashioned into a pillow top. "Bow Tie Quilt." Designed by Jane McGown Flynn. House of Price / Charco pattern. Hooked by Suzanne S. Hamer. Illinois. 1999. 14" x 14". *Courtesy of Suzanne S. Hamer.*

"Color Diamond" offers a rainbow palette. "My philosophy was to show how colors interact as they intersect one another." Designed and hooked by Sharon Saknit. California. 2004. 20" x 20". *Courtesy of Sharon Saknit.*

A miniature burst of color. "Color Proportion Study." Designed and hooked by Suzanne S. Hamer. Illinois. 2004. 6" x 6". *Courtesy of Suzanne S. Hamer.*

Color-filled triangles and a partial diamond full of curlicues are the backdrop for a branch of golden stars and pair of fanciful birds. "Stars and Swirls." Designed by Monica Jones. Hooked by Susan Naples. California. 2004. 24" x 37.5". *Courtesy of Susan Naples.*

A piece of fabric was inspiration for this rug's color scheme. "Antique Geometric." Adapted from an antique rug pattern. Maker unknown. Hooked by Sharon Saknit. California. 2001. 23" x 33". *Courtesy of Sharon Saknit.*

Detail of "Antique Geometric." *Courtesy of Sharon Saknit.*

"Crazy Rug." Bright colors play against subdued shades, forming a crazy quilt-like collage. Beverly Conway Designs. Hooked by Susan Naples. California. 2003. 23" x 38". *Courtesy of Susan Naples.*

An organic chemist by trade, Tatijanna Tonshina learned how to hook rugs in a class taught in Moscow by California hooking artist and teacher Gene Shepherd. "She continues to create her own designs and is always glad to share the art form with friends and neighbors in Moscow." "Russian Snowflake" is now owned by Gene Shepherd. Designed and hooked by Tatijanna Tonshina. Moscow, Russia. 2003. 31" x 31". *Courtesy of Tatijanna Tonshina and Gene Shepherd.*

In addition to strips of woolen fabric, Suzanne Hamer incorporated small bits of light blue silk from her husband's tie collection into "Little Echo." Designed by Jane McGown Flynn. House of Price / Charco pattern. Hooked by Suzanne S. Hamer. Illinois. 1999. 26.5" x 19". *Courtesy of Suzanne S. Hamer.*

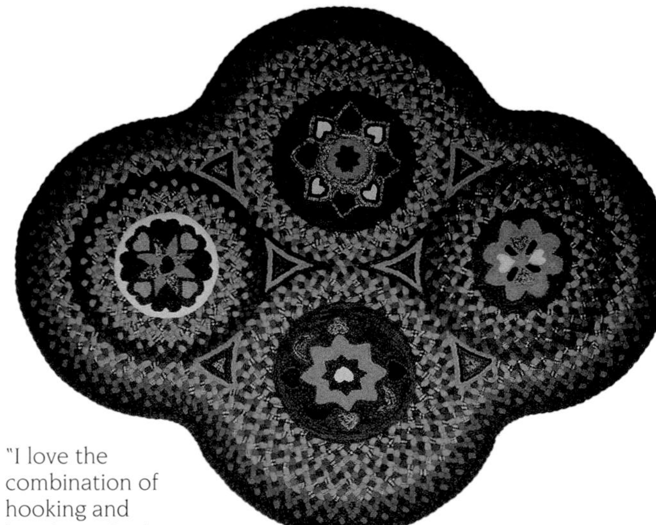

"I love the combination of hooking and braiding—both can be completed in various shapes and sizes. This was started as a single chair pad. Because I loved the colors, it grew into a rug as I experimented with the ways to join circles." The four circles were adapted from appliquéd Baltimore Album quilt patterns. "Sea Foam." Designed and hooked by Kris McDermet. Vermont. 2004. 38" x 48". *Courtesy of Kris McDermet.*

"I knew this rug was going to be an entry-way rug. Consequently, I wanted a pattern and colors that wouldn't show the dirt. I also wanted to use up scraps. I saw a helix design somewhere and thought it would be fun to try to use it as a basic pattern. The background color was the result of mixing all my leftover dyes together and over-dyeing wools of many different colors and textures. The border uses all the colors in the main part of the rug and I got rid of a lot of small pieces that I would have thrown away. When I put the rug on the floor in front of the door my son was horrified! 'Everyone will wipe their feet on it.' That's what I made it for." "Stanwood." Designed and hooked by Peggy Stanilonis. Vermont. 2002. 33" x 35". *Courtesy of Peggy Stanilonis.*

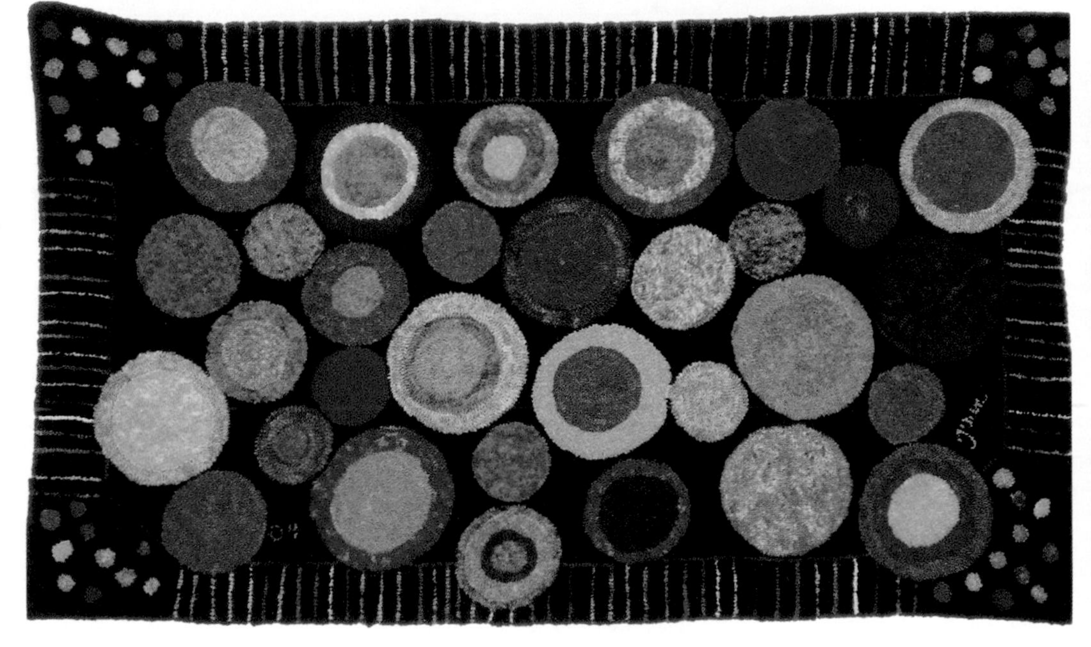

Bright, vibrant and going "Around in Circles." Designed and hooked by Joan Payton. Georgia. 2004. 30" x 51". *Courtesy of Joan Payton.*

"Urbano." A modern look at geometric elements. Adapted from a sketch drawn by Bill Payton. Hooked by Joan Payton. Georgia. 2002. 33" x 23". *Courtesy of Joan Payton.*

Braided or hooked? This braided look-a-like rug was actually hooked using the "worms" or left over woolen strips from other rug projects. "The Worm Runner." Designed and hooked by Thelma P. Kirkhoff. Pennsylvania. 1999. 24" x 79". *Courtesy of Thelma P. Kirkhoff.*

John Flournoy—Lewes, Delaware

Although John Flournoy has no formal art training, his hooked works have been exhibited at art shows and in galleries along the Eastern seaboard, have appeared in numerous publications, received honors from the Carnegie Center for Art and History in Indiana, and attracted an enthusiastic audience in Tokyo, Japan. John, who divides his time between homes in Maryland and Delaware, began hooking rugs in 1994, under the direction of Maryland's noted hooking artist, Roslyn Logsdon. "Since starting to hook eleven years ago I have learned to look at everything differently. Hooking has opened my eyes to color, light, shadow, and perspective. In the past, I had taken all that for granted. Now I pick up a leaf and study its colors and shape, then look at a tree or shrub to see how all of it works together. I do the same with the image of a building or a person's face."

A bit of a Renaissance man, John buys, sells, and collects antiques, as well as doing furniture refinishing, chair caning, decorative and faux painting, and gardening. "I will continue to hook and try new things to stretch my abilities. Maybe I'll hook an abstract? Maybe a self-portrait?"

A captured moment. Hooking artist John Flournoy's use of light and shadow allows us an impressionist view of a woman tending her Maine garden. "Kennebunkport Garden." Adapted from a painting by Abbott Fuller Graves (1859-1936). Hooked by John Flournoy. Delaware. 1997. 31" x 22.5". *Courtesy of Tom Baxivanos and Henry Fountain.*

"Letters from Camp Rehoboth." Inspiration comes from many sources. Adapted with permission from the cover of the magazine of the same name. Hooked by John Flournoy. Delaware. 1999. 31.5" x 23.5". *Courtesy of John Flournoy.*

The early days of airline travel. John Flournoy's attention to detail is noteworthy. Masterfully hooked are the subtle shadows and creases found on and in the clothing of the gathered crowd. "Reminisce." Adapted with permission from a photograph in the magazine *Reminisce*. Hooked by John Flournoy. Delaware. 2000. 30" x 45.5". *Courtesy of John Flournoy.*

Sepia tones recall a bygone age. "Steel Workers." Adapted from an old postcard. Hooked by John Flournoy. Delaware. 2001. 16.5" x 24". *Courtesy of John Flournoy.*

Meticulously hooked from the detail of the front porch railings to the bend of the rocker's wicker. We observe this Florida home from an interesting angle. "Old Key West." Designed and hooked by John Flournoy. Delaware. 2002. 19.5" x 28.5". *Courtesy of John Flournoy.*

Lined up and asking to be hooked: a trio of the Sunshine State's vintage beauties. "Old Key West II." Designed and hooked by John Flournoy. Delaware. 2003. 25" x 50". *Courtesy of John Flournoy.*

A hooked photographic image of "Pennsylvania Barns." Designed and hooked by John Flournoy. Delaware. 2003. 17.5" x 48". *Courtesy of John Flournoy.*

Steeped in European charm. Adapted from a postcard of Paris. "L'Hotel de Cluny." Hooked by John Flournoy. Delaware. 2004. 27.5" x 23". *Courtesy of John Flournoy.*

Tiger Ladies

In the fall of 2004 (October 18- November 12), The Nassau Club of Princeton, New Jersey, hosted "The Tigers of Princeton Hooked Rug Show and Sale." Initiated by fiber artists interested in marketing their work, the exhibit and sale also served as a fundraiser for a local women's shelter.

In the words of "Tiger" organizer Claudia Casebolt, "We decided to create rugs with a single theme, a theme that could be explored in endless ways, in different styles of design and hooking—primitive, realistic, impressionistic and geometric—with a wide range of color palettes. The tiger was an easy choice; as the mascot for Princeton University nearby, it would be popular in town and at the university."

Fourteen took the challenge and created tiger-related hooked art that was met by an enthusiastic and buying audience. Twenty per cent of the proceeds from sales resulted in a generous check for Woman's Space. Those who participated received a booklet containing photographs of the exhibited rugs and a certificate declaring official "Tiger Lady" status.

Bold, bright hooked letters declare the name of the university and its location in New Jersey. "Princeton." Designed and hooked by Susan McDonald. Massachusetts. 2004. 17" x 36". *Courtesy of Susan McDonald.*

"'Rajah' was drawn to appear as though he were looking off to the right and turned to face you as you approached him, disturbing him." This handsome tiger portrait was sold and is now in the private collection of the president of the Princeton University graduating class of 1923. Designed and hooked by Trish Becker. New Jersey. 2004. 25.5" x 25.5". *Courtesy of Trish Becker–The Woolery, Inc.*

"Tumbling Tigers." Round and round they go. Adapted from "Tumbling Cats" design by Dahlov Ipcar. Hooked by Claudia Casebolt. New Jersey. 2004. 30.5" x 45". *Courtesy of Claudia Casebolt.*

"I wanted to hook a rug that said Princeton without the words. So in addition to the tiger, I hooked a black squirrel, because they are common on campus and in the Princeton area. The ivy vine suggests that the animals are in the Ivy League." "Dillon and Palmer." Designed and hooked by Roberta Smith. New Jersey. 2004. 19.5" x 29". *Courtesy of Roberta Smith.*

"My original design was to hook a tiger lying on a field of grasses. As I was working on it one day, I thought back to beautiful fall afternoons, many years ago, when I was at Palmer Stadium. That thought gave me the inspiration—the tiger was meant to be the football field." "Hold That Tiger." Designed and hooked by Pat Eldridge. Vermont. 2004. 35" x 25". *Courtesy of Pat Eldridge.*

Tiger-like ribs cut across brilliant shocks of chartreuse. A decorative border complements the abstract image. "Jadwin In the Grass." Designed and hooked by Marilyn Robinson. New Jersey. 2004. 25" x 49". *Courtesy of Marilyn Robinson.*

Resting in a pool of reflected jungle lights. "Carnegie, the Lake Tiger." Designed and hooked by Heidi H. Blair. New Jersey. 2004. 25" x 27". *Courtesy of Heidi H. Blair.*

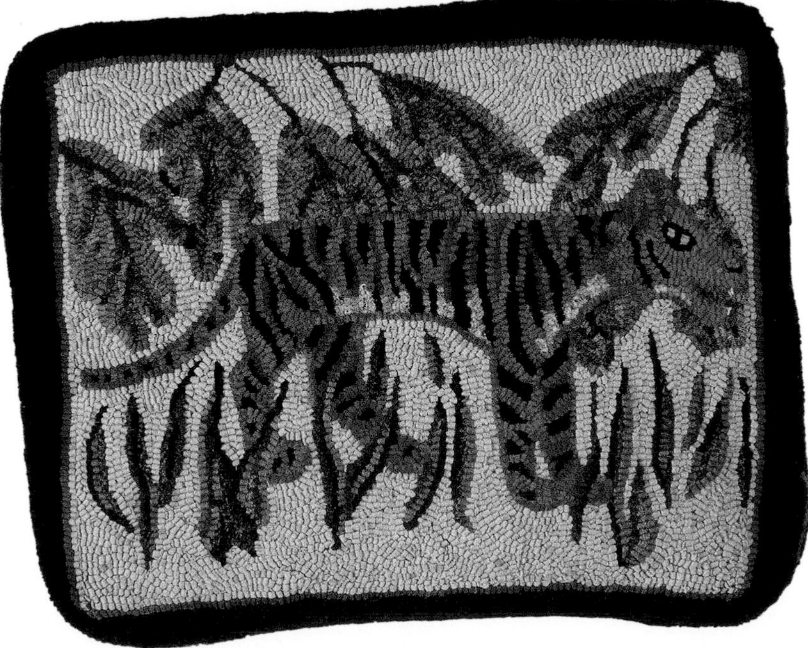

A place for paws. "Tiger Foot Stool." Designed and hooked by Claudia Casebolt. New Jersey. 2004. 13.5" x 16.5". *Courtesy of Claudia Casebolt.*

A seated tiger surveys his domain. Rug hooking artist Phyllis Hamel left the date 19—blank. Upon purchase, she would hook in the year of the new owner's graduating class. The striking piece was purchased by The Ivy Club of Princeton and personalized with the date of the club's founding. "Ivy Tiger." Designed and hooked by Phyllis Hamel. New Jersey. 2004. 30" x 22.5". *Courtesy of Phyllis Hamel.*

"Tiger, Tiger." Stealthily gazing out from jungle foliage and poetic verse. Inspired by William Blake's poem. Designed and hooked by Barbara Dalrymple Lugg. New Jersey. 2004. 23.5" x 17.5". *Courtesy of Barbara Dalrymple Lugg.*

Oversized fanciful leaves form a backdrop against a young tiger, years shy of being regarded as the "old guard." "The Young Guard." Designed and hooked by Susan McDonald. Massachusetts. 2004. 9.5" x 15". *Courtesy of Susan McDonald.*

"I was hesitant to participate after I saw all the beautiful tigers evolving and I felt I had to do something other than an 'actual' tiger. With my preference for geometrics, creating this design was a natural for me. It now hangs in my daughter's office at a private school in Virginia whose mascot is the tiger." "Firestone Tiger." Designed and hooked by Peggie Cunningham. New Jersey. 2004. 42" x 25". *Courtesy of Peggie Cunningham.*

Mother and cubs at play. A colorful border frames the captured moment. Adapted from an antique rug. "Tiger Family." Lib Callaway pattern / Hook Nook. Hooked by Margaret Lutz. New Jersey. 2004. 27" x 42". *Courtesy of Margaret Lutz.*

On the prowl. "Zeus." Adapted from a 1983 *International Wildlife Magazine* photograph by Erwin and Peggy Bauer, now both deceased. Permission to adapt the photograph was granted by their son, Parker Bauer. Hooked by Joyce Combs. New Jersey. 2004. 36" x 18". *Courtesy of Joyce Combs.*

Cocktails anyone? A decorating must-have for all Princeton University students, alumni, employees, and residents of the community. "Tiger Paw Coasters." Designed and hooked by Margaret Brightbill. New Jersey. 2004. Each piece 4.5" x 4.5". *Courtesy of Margaret Brightbill.*

"Princeton Tigers." Lurking in Henri Rousseau inspired flora and foliage, five tigers— some of original design, some recognizable from antique rugs—protect Nassau Hall, Princeton University's oldest building. Designed and hooked by Pandy Goodbody. Massachusetts. 2004. 31" x 45". *Courtesy of Pandy Goodbody.*

Hooked Houses

Loop by loop, hooked houses are built. Structurally small but heartwarming to all.

"Length of Houses" was hooked on a loosely woven piece of woolen fabric, hand-dyed to resemble grass and sky. Designed and hooked by Joyce Krueger. Wisconsin. 2000. 9.5" x 40." *Courtesy of Joyce Krueger.*

Charming simplicity. Hooked houses in a row. "The Blue House is Mine." Adapted from a quilt pattern. Hooked by Polly Reinhart. Pennsylvania. 2004. 21" x 27". *Courtesy of Polly Reinhart.*

Decorative lamb's tongue borders and heart corners frame "Bless This House." Designed by Edyth O'Neill. Woolley Fox pattern. Hooked by Shirley S. Lothrop. Maine. 1997. 26" x 34". *Courtesy of Shirley S. Lothrop.*

Geometric-shaped trees flank a "House by the Side of the Road." Designed and hooked by Betsy Gerakaris. Connecticut. 2003. 26" x 36". *Courtesy of Betsy Gerakaris.*

"Claire's Cottage." A storybook house hooked for granddaughter, Claire. Designed and hooked by Beth Kempf. Connecticut. 2000. 29" x 37". *Courtesy of Beth Kempf.*

Sweet Grass Baskets

Sweet grass baskets are synonymous with Charleston, South Carolina, and are part of the heritage of those who live in the region. Since the wild growing grass is becoming difficult to find and harvest (due to the increased building in the area), and few young people are interested in continuing the time-consuming tradition, the number of baskets being made is limited. "This rug is my way of showing appreciation to the wonderful basket makers and their hard work to produce such beautiful art." "Charleston Sweet Grass Baskets." Adapted from a photograph taken by Charles Johnston. Hooked by Valerie A. Johnston. North Carolina. 2003. 26.5" x 33.5". *Courtesy of Valerie A. Johnston.*

Flowers and Fruit Contained

Rug hookers not only enjoy hooking flowers and fruit, they also like to be creative with the receptacles that hold them.

A series of geometric, floral, and abstract patterns draw attention to a trio of lollypop flowers held in a simple elongated container. Shades of indigo blue and rust recall early hand-dyed fabrics. "Old Chatham." Lib Callaway pattern / Hook Nook. Hooked by Jane M. Bescherer. Connecticut. 2003. 34" x 36". *Courtesy of Jane M. Bescherer.*

Meandering vines protrude from a scallop-edged, diamond motif decorative pot. The written words, "fortitude, endurance, faith, and perseverance" blend into the eclectic background. Note the antiquated use of the word wrought…to work into shape artistically. "My Wisdom." Designed and hooked by Jane M. Bescherer. Connecticut. 2002. 33" x 52". *Courtesy of Jane M. Bescherer.*

"Hat and Flowers." "I love primitive designs that make no sense—funky changing backgrounds, unbalanced elements, high contrast, and bright colors." Designed and hooked by Jule Marie Smith. New York. 2004. 16" x 25". *Courtesy of Jule Marie Smith.*

Fantasy flowers—some top heavy, some not—spring forth from a diminutive striped container. A series of polychrome borders compete for attention. "#3 Border Series." Designed and hooked by Judy Quintman. North Carolina. 2004. 28.5" x 37.5". *Courtesy of Judy Quintman.*

After taking hooking classes at Vermont's Shelburne Museum, this artist thought it only natural to hook "Flowers for Shelburne." In primitive fashion, a sturdy receptacle dominates the scene and secures a sparse arrangement. Designed and hooked by Donna Lee Beaudoin. Vermont. 2001. 20" x 28". *Courtesy of Donna Lee Beaudoin.*

A stylized basket supports sturdy stalks of florets and foliage. Note the decorative jonquil-like stars. "Flowers and Stars." Barbara Brown pattern. Hooked by Shirley S. Lothrop. Maine. 1998. 14.5" x 30". *Courtesy of Shirley S. Lothrop.*

Emerging from a striped pot, colorful "Primitive Posies" bring a note of cheer. Multicolored stripes form a haphazard linear frame. Pat Cross pattern. Hooked by Joan Mohrmann. New York. 2004. 26" x 30". *Courtesy of Joan Mohrmann.*

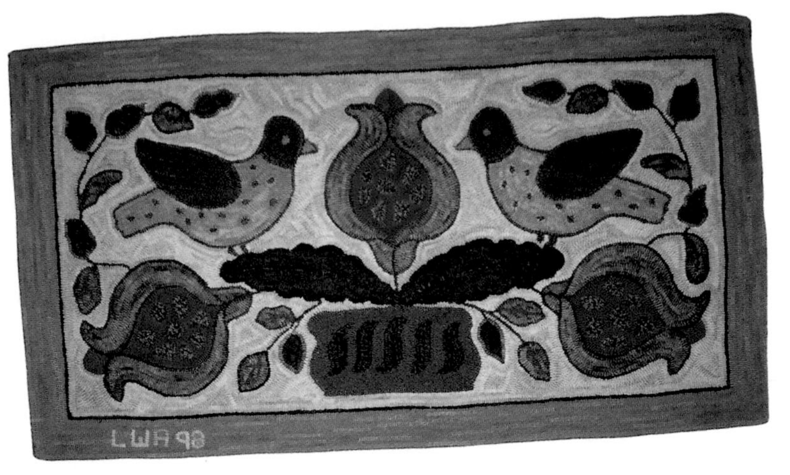

A rather plain pot, enhanced with simple S curve motifs, secures a trio of oversized pomegranates and a pair of speckled birds. "Buds and Pomegranates." Designed by Edyth O'Neill. Woolley Fox pattern. Hooked by Lee Abrego. New Hampshire. 1998. 37" x 67". *Courtesy of Lee Abrego.*

Boughs of winter berries and buds collected in a star studded container form a pleasing "Winter Floral." Designed and hooked by Lisanne Miller. Maine. 2004. 9" x 18". *Courtesy of Lisanne Miller.*

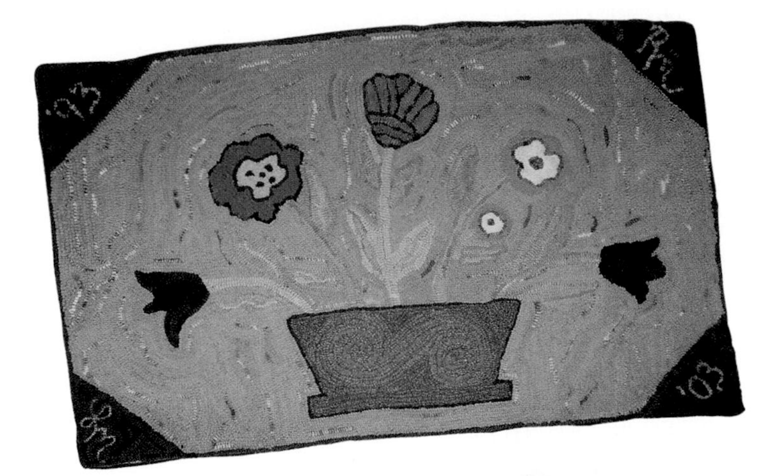

"This rug was designed for our tenth wedding anniversary. The idea was to have the rug look 'antique' as it came off the frame. The two dates are in remembrance of our ten years together and my husband even hooked his own initials! I ran out of background and had to fill in with a second color—just like marriage…a give and take situation." The vessel supporting the flowers displays a curlicue design also symbolic of the ups and downs of every relationship. "Ten Years of Wedded Bliss." Designed and hooked by Lisanne Miller. Maine. 2003. 24" x 36". *Courtesy of Lisanne Miller.*

A woven basket hosts a lively arrangement of fruit, flowers, and fluttering butterflies. "Crewel Sampler." Jacqueline Designs pattern. Hooked by Barbara Mabbs Robinson. New Hampshire. 1999. 26" x 36". *Courtesy of Barbara Mabbs Robinson.*

An ornate urn, complete with tasseled festoon, supports an "18th Century Delft" floral motif. Patsy Becker pattern. Hooked by Paige Osborn Stoep. New York. 2004. 28" x 44". *Courtesy of Paige Osborn Stoep.*

Reminiscent of a painted still life; the epitome of grace and elegance. A Wedgwood-blue compote, placed on carefully draped fabric, holds a lush array of blossoms, foliage, and grapes. "Blythe Shoals." Prairie Craft House pattern. Hooked by Carla Fortney. California. 2004. 31" x 38". *Courtesy of Carla Fortney.*

Early theorem paintings were often fashioned on velvet using a series of stencils. This "Fruit Theorem" comes complete with a scalloped frame. Designed by Edyth O'Neill. Woolley Fox pattern. Hooked by Tricia Travis. Texas. 2001. 30" x 51". *Courtesy of Tricia Travis.*

Another version of "Fruit Theorem." Designed by Edyth O'Neill. Woolley Fox pattern. Hooked by Edyth O'Neill. Texas. 2001. 30" x 51". *Courtesy of Edyth O'Neill.*

A fruit basket hooked in earthy tones was a birthday gift for Betsy Wagner, the rug maker's daughter. "Fruit Basket." Designed by Warren Kimble. Woolley Fox pattern. Hooked by Polly Reinhart. Pennsylvania. 2003. 26" x 35". *Courtesy of Polly Reinhart.*

"Fruit Basket with Crow." A 3/4 polychrome scalloped edge adds a finishing touch. Wavy lines, of a similar palette, rest behind the decorative container and complete the outer edge border. Designed by Jule Marie Smith and Suzanne Hamer. Hooked by Suzanne S. Hamer. Illinois. 2001. 18.5" x 25". *Courtesy of Suzanne S. Hamer.*

Hooked Portraits

Portraits, whether realistic, impressionistic, or abstract, are yet another way for rug hookers to express their creativity. Hooking artists use their hook and strips of woolen fabric as a portrait artist would use his brush and paint.

Imaginary women share the joys of universal sisterhood. "Soul Sisters." Designed and hooked by Joan Payton. Georgia. 2005. 33.5" x 28". *Courtesy of Joan Payton.*

A favorite old song served as inspiration for this hooked vignette of three ocean-loving sisters on vacation at North Carolina's Outer Banks. "A Perfect Day." Designed and hooked by Ruth Hennessey. New York. 2002. 35" x 43.5". *Courtesy of Ruth Hennessey*.

Beach umbrella stripes frame anxious youngsters as they anticipate a day of fun. "Grandkids at the Beach." Designed and hooked by Judy Quintman. North Carolina. 2004. 15" x 26". *Courtesy of Judy Quintman.*

Painted nails, colorful frock, and a sun-shading hat, complete with attached hooked flower, makes for a stylish image. "Gardening." Beverly Conway Designs. Hooked by Susan Bryan. Iowa. 2004. 35" x 21". *Courtesy of Susan Bryan.*

"This piece was started in Diane Phillips' 'Women With Attitude' class at the Green Mountain Guild workshop at the Shelburne Museum in Vermont. I asked Diane if I could sit in on the class since my plane did not leave until evening. After just a few minutes, I knew I wanted to take all three days of the class. When Diane said 'yes,' I rushed to make the arrangements—change the plane, change the car, get a hotel, and make the most important phone call home. I thought, 'I'd walk over hot coals for Diane.' Back in class I drew 'Glorious Grammy' directly on the linen foundation and started hooking." Designed and hooked by Sharon L. Townsend. Iowa. 2000. 48" x 30". *Courtesy of Sharon L. Townsend.*

"Several years ago, my mother was coming out of the hospital just as our annual rug show was about to start. While we were looking through her closet to bring clothes to my house for her recovery, I found a pair of red, open-toed, high-heeled sandals. I'm sure my mother hadn't worn them since 1970 at least. My mother, who was eighty-four at the time, was sitting on the bed watching. I said, 'Mom, should a woman using a walker wear these?' My mother's response was a hearty laugh. Her wonderful attitude inspired my subject for a class I took at the rug show with Diane Phillips called 'Women with Attitude.' Both my mother and I use the 'Power of Red Shoes' as our code for 'we can get through anything.'" Note the lace collar and button embellishments. Designed and hooked by Suzanne Dirmaier. Vermont. 2003. 48" x 29". *Courtesy of Suzanne Dirmaier.*

"Looking at my ten granddaughters, 'Meg' seems to have the most distinguishing characteristics. One-quarter of her genes are Peruvian and she inherited lovely, curly hair that can be unruly at times. I tried to capture her wonderful crown on one of those days in a hooking." "Meg." Designed and hooked by Sally D'Albora. Maryland. 2004. 16.5" x 18". *Courtesy of Sally D'Albora.*

Abby, all dressed in blue. Inspired by a photograph of her then two-year-old granddaughter, Emily Robertson captured the toddler's innate curiosity. "Abby with Orange Polka Dots." Designed and hooked by Emily Robertson. Massachusetts. 2004. 22" x 31". *Courtesy of Emily Robertson.*

"I wanted to play the face game and try my hand at hooking faces. The fun part is that the personality of the face comes as you hook, totally independent of any plan. 'Magda' is gentle yet strong and has lived some life." Designed and hooked by Jule Marie Smith. New York. 2004. 15" x 15". *Courtesy of Jule Marie Smith.*

"I'm trying to break out of my own box with color and 'Rosalita' is wilder than 'Magda'—saucier, fiery. I prefer the play of warm colors. Again, she became who she is through the hooking process. I feel compelled to try more and more faces!" Designed and hooked by Jule Marie Smith. New York. 2004. 15" x 15". *Courtesy of Jule Marie Smith.*

"In a class I was teaching, I hooked 'Streetwise' as a demonstration of how to hook features in a face. I would hook a feature such as eyes and then the participants would hook eyes in their rugs. Then the nose, mouth, ear, etc. 'Streetwise' was referred to as 'demo woman' until she was completed and later renamed." Designed and hooked by Diane Phillips. New York. 2004. 16" x 14". *Courtesy of Diane Phillips.*

A single piece of woolen fabric, dyed for a fiber study group, influenced the coloration of this "self portrait of sorts." The hand-dyed shade of blue was "Position 10" on the color wheel, hence the name. Designed and hooked by Linda Rae Coughlin. New Jersey. 2003. 19" x 16". *Courtesy of Linda Rae Coughlin.*

"This rug reminds me of the terrible tragedy of spousal abuse. It was completed and hanging on the wall when the black eye and swollen lip became apparent. I hope she stops making excuses for the bum and leaves to make a new life." "He Doesn't Mean to Do It." Designed and hooked by Diane Phillips. New York. 2004. 14" x 13". *Courtesy of Diane Phillips.*

"No real story. Just the joy of working with lovely burnished colors—eggplants and caramels and deep browns." "Remembering." Designed and hooked by Diane Phillips. New York. 14" x 14". *Courtesy of Diane Phillips.*

"'Pimento' is a living, loving, four-and-a-half pound Chihuahua that is my constant companion. He is now gray from old age but has bright color in his spirit. He is lion-hearted and loving. His look in this rug says, 'Pick me up.'" Designed and hooked by Diane Phillips. New York. 2004. 21" x 23". *Courtesy of Diane Phillips*

In response to a "Faces" hooking class taught by Vermont hooking artist Burma Cassidy, Diane Phillips took the challenge to create something she had never done before. She outlined bold planes of color while fashioning an impressionistic portrait. "Mediterranean Man." Designed and hooked by Diane Phillips. New York. 2004. 18" x 14". *Courtesy of Diane Phillips.*

Burma Cassidy's "Faces" class inspired many hooking artists, including Jean MacQuiddy. Planes of color divide her abstract "Self Portrait." Designed and hooked by Jean E. MacQuiddy. Massachusetts. 2004. 36" x 24". *Courtesy of Jean E. MacQuiddy.*

"This is my first hooked face. It happened as a result of a class on 'Faces,' which I took with Burma Cassidy. I am now entranced with faces." In addition to hooking with strips of woolen fabric, the artist also incorporated lengths of ribbon. "Nina." Designed and hooked by Barbara Held. Vermont. 2004. 42" x 38". *Courtesy of Barbara Held.*

"She's the person who goes on living with all the passion and 'Courage' needed in our world today." Designed and hooked by Burma Cassidy. Vermont. 2004. 23.5" x 16.5". *Courtesy of Burma Cassidy.*

A common sense verse, voiced by actress Katherine Hepburn, frames a worldly soul adorned in vivid attire. "Paddle Your Own Canoe." Designed and hooked by Barbara Held. Vermont. 2004. 15" x 15". *Courtesy of Barbara Held.*

"Burma Cassidy offered a weekend face workshop that was magical. She had us dye a mixture of light, medium, and dark colors and those were the palettes I choose from. My plan was to do a more realistic face than I had done before in an artistic manner, not worrying about the color so much as the value of the color. That freed me to use a mixture of colors. The whole piece was 'Uncharted Water' for me, as well as being an uncharted time in my life." Designed and hooked by Sharon L. Townsend. Iowa. 2004. 38" x 32". Walnut and cherry hand-carved and painted frame crafted by Jim Lilly. *Courtesy of Sharon L. Townsend.*

Detail of "Uncharted Water." *Courtesy of Sharon L. Townsend.*

Detail of "Uncharted Water" shows a portion of the unique walnut and cherry hand-carved and painted frame crafted by Jim Lilly. *Courtesy of Sharon L. Townsend.*

"Woman of Strength" is a small portrait study for "The Bass," a life-size hooked orchestra series. Designed and hooked by Rae Reynolds Harrell. Vermont. 2004. 18" x 15". *Courtesy of Rae Reynolds Harrell.*

An Elizabeth Taylor look-a-like. She was then and she is now. "Me, Before My Hair Turned Silver." Designed and hooked by Gloria Reynolds. Vermont. 2002. 26" x 18". *Courtesy of Gloria Reynolds.*

"As a painter myself, I have been greatly influenced by the work of van Gogh. The boldness and colors of his works have intrigued and fascinated me. He died never knowing his greatness. I honor his memory with this small token." "van Gogh's Agony." Designed and hooked by Gloria Reynolds. Vermont. 2004. 15" x 13". *Courtesy of Gloria Reynolds.*

A series of profiles face a positive approach to life. "The Verbs of Growth." Designed and hooked by Diane S. Kelly. Vermont. 2004. 19" x 26". Courtesy of *Diane* S. *Kelly*.

"This piece (a two-sided pillow) represents my life 'Before and After' learning rug hooking. The gray monochromatic side is my 'before,' while the colorful side illustrates the color, vitality, and joy rug hooking has brought me." Designed by Laura Pierce. Hooked by Sharon Saknit. California. 2004. 11" x 11". *Courtesy of Sharon Saknit*.

A dream-like portrait of a young woman at peace not only with the earth, sea, and sky, but also with those she holds dear. This is the artist's first hooked rug. "Cherished Heart." Designed and hooked by Eugenie S. Delaney. Vermont. 2001. 42" x 32". *Courtesy of Eugenie S. Delaney.*

Guardian angels, one shocked and one displeased, watch over the two who started it all. "Adam and Eve Sampler." Designed by Edyth O'Neill. Woolley Fox pattern. Hooked by Tricia Travis. Texas. 2001. 33" x 52". *Courtesy of Tricia Travis.*

"She's all set…purse filled with $$ and a lucky lemon on her head." "Lady with Lemon Going to Vegas." Designed and hooked by Burma Cassidy. Vermont. 2004. 23" x 8". *Courtesy of Burma Cassidy.*

Right:
"Fallen Angel: Self Portrait." A once somber gravestone rubbing is transformed into a whimsical image of a rug hooker. "Overhead Angel." Vermont Folk Rugs pattern. Hooked by Carol Lea Anderson. Pennsylvania. 2004. 11" x 34". *Courtesy of Carol Lea Anderson.*

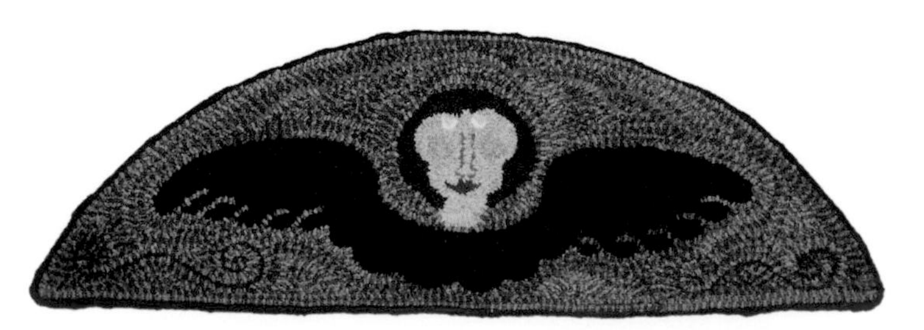

Photographic Images

Cameras capture the moments in time that rug makers love to hook.

Seventy-five folks dressed in Easter finery. The gathering, which includes members of the artist's family, is a compilation of several 1940s photographs of the Fairfield Church in Richmond, Virginia, and a local homecoming celebration. "Homecoming at Fairfield Church, circa 1940." Designed and hooked by Sarah Province. Maryland. 2002. 20" x 25". *Courtesy of Sarah Province.*

Generations come together for a hooked "Family Portrait." Adapted from a Christmas photograph. Hooked by Jan Seavey. New Hampshire. 1996. 18" x 30". *Courtesy of Jan Seavey.*

"'Dad and Hoyt' was adapted from an old family photo of my father and his brother when they were young linemen for the Pennsylvania Electric Company, circa 1920s." Hooked by Ruth Hennessey. New York. 2001. 15" x 12". *Courtesy of Ruth Hennessey.*

"There is a tale my father recounts about taking my mother to Paris after World War II, the year before I was born. My mom was very excited. She bought a new outfit and went to get her hair done. 'Mom—Off to Paris—1945' was adapted from the photo my father took just as she left the hairdressers." Note the addition of buttons to the hooked blouse. Hooked by Annie Wilson. California. 2004. 18" x 14". *Courtesy of Annie Wilson.*

A third generation returns to a favorite vacation spot in Maine. "Matthew and Andrew at Moose Pond." Adapted from a photograph. Hooked by Judy Fresk. Connecticut. 2002. 33" x 33". *Courtesy of Judy Fresk.*

"The scene depicts a child focused on his own action with his mother nearby. Her closeness and gesture offer an emotional and physical support that he may rely on. Knowing this, he reaches up to grasp her hand as a tool for his own purpose. This reassuring grasp provides him with an opportunity to explore the world, and, in part, allows them to go their own ways while still connected." The hooked vignette depicts the artist's two year old son. "Mother and Child." Adapted from a photograph. Hooked by Susan Higgins. California. 1997. 15" x 22". *Courtesy of Susan Higgins.*

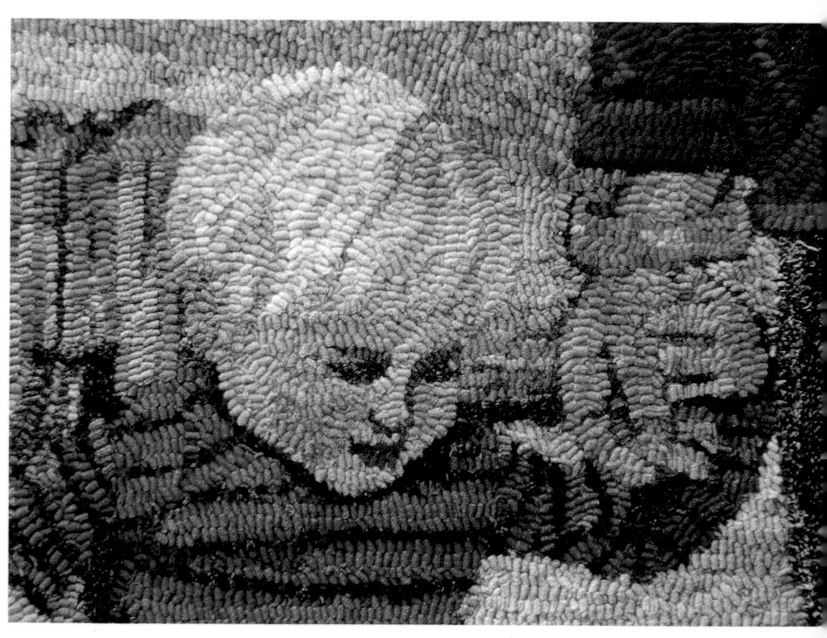

Detail of "Mother and Child." *Courtesy of Susan Higgins.*

A hooked prized possession. "My father took a photo of me when I was four years old. I adapted it for this rug—I have to give him summer custody of the rug every year." "My Reflection." Hooked by Jen Lavoie. Vermont. 2002. 39" x 28". *Courtesy of Jen Lavoie.*

A determined four-year-old leaves home. Adapted from a black and white photograph of the artist as a youngster. "Running Away." Designed and hooked by Diane S. Kelly. Vermont. 2001. 21" x 16". *Courtesy of Diane S. Kelly.*

Something Fishy

The days are gone when images of our finned friends were relegated to wilderness cabins and backyard sheds. Fish are swimming upstream and making a big splash in the world of decorating divas. Rug hookers, always on the leading edge of style and fashion, realize this and have hooked some reel beauties.

Swimming along in a sea of colored bubbles. "Fish With Bubbles." Designed and hooked by Polly Reinhart. Pennsylvania. 2002. 19" x 24". *Courtesy of Polly Reinhart.*

A trio of colorful finned friends, hooked for four grandchildren who love to fish, swim in opposite directions. Using a favorite prayer rug motif, Judy Fresk incorporated a water theme in the background of "Susi" and also added a wave-like border. Designed and hooked by Judy Fresk. Connecticut. 2004. 42" x 30". *Courtesy of Judy Fresk.*

"I have worked on a charter fishing boat for the past nine years. I am particularly fond of bass. Over the years I have seen the population increase dramatically due to catch and release practices and conservation efforts to increase the numbers of these beautiful fish." "Striped Bass." Designed and hooked by Pam Evans. Rhode Island. 2002. 33" x 44". *Courtesy of Pam Evans.*

Detail of "Striped Bass." *Courtesy of Pam Evans.*

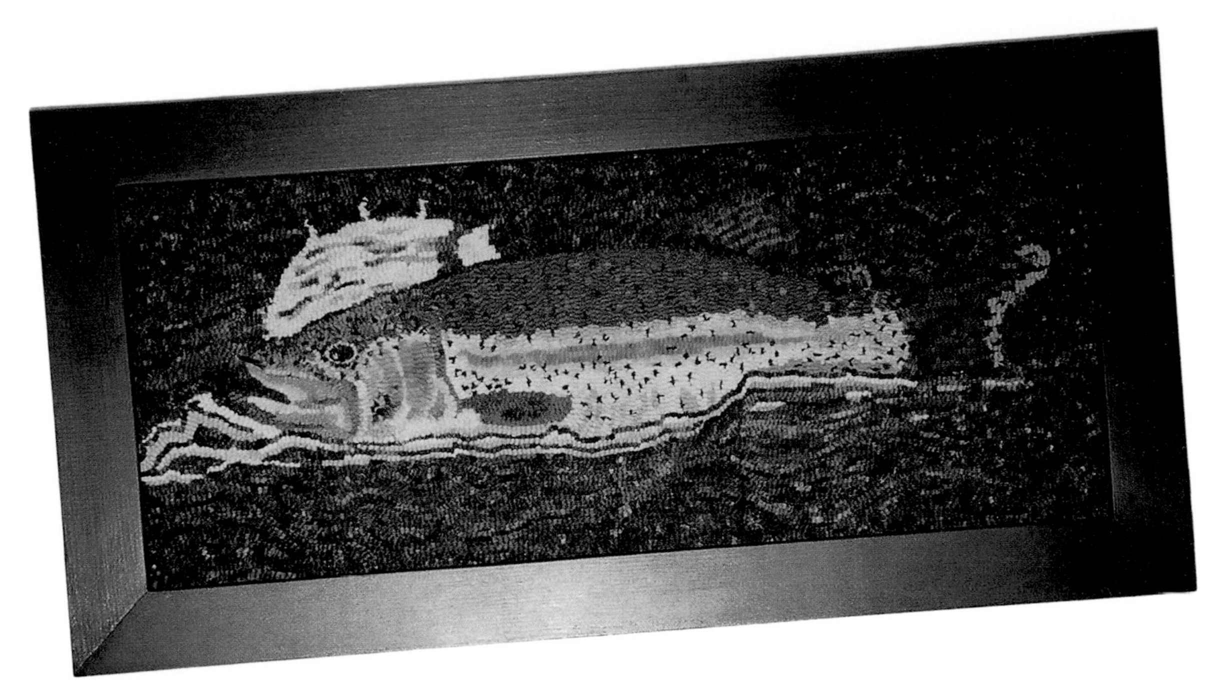

Not only did Charlotte Hefford hook this "Rainbow Trout" for her husband to commemorate their trip out West, she also took up fly fishing. Adapted from photographs. Designed by Sarah Guiliani. Hooked by Charlotte Hefford. Maine. 2003. 9.5" x 22.5". *Courtesy of Charlotte Hefford.*

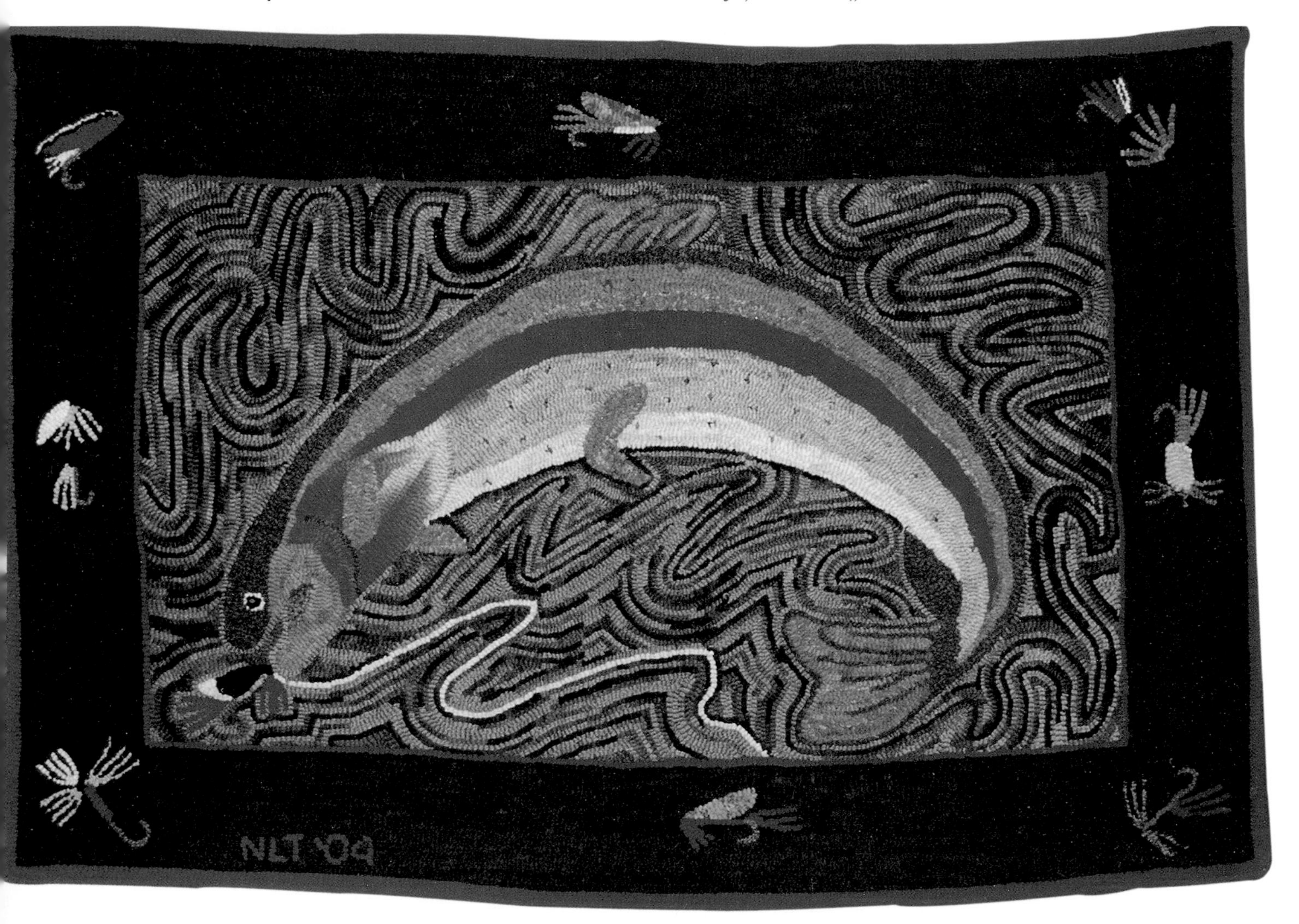

Framed by flies and about to be caught by one, a handsome "Rainbow Trout" leaps across undulating waters. Designed and hooked by Nancy Taylor. Maine. 2004. 25" x 36". *Courtesy of Nancy Taylor.*

Hookers' Tribute to Other Artists

Inspired by other artists, rug hookers often pay tribute to those they admire.

"Inspired by works of art since childhood, it was only natural for me to hook an impressionistic painting by van Gogh." "van Gogh's Starry Night." Adapted from the painting by Vincent van Gogh. Made into a pattern by Rae Reynolds Harrell. Hooked by Diane Burgess. Vermont. 2003. 36" x 48". *Courtesy of Diane Burgess.*

"I hooked this rug for my daughter, who is in love with paintings by Vincent van Gogh." Finely cut strips of woolen fabric were used to replicate the artist's brush strokes. "Café Terrace at Night." Adapted from the painting by Vincent van Gogh. Hooked by Joanne Thomason. Iowa. 2004. 30" x 40". *Courtesy of Joanne Thomason.*

"The 'Iris' is my favorite flower and I have grown them in all of my gardens. I am still most impressed with the blue iris, perhaps because they were the ones my father grew, or perhaps because of the breathtakingly beautiful portrayal of the blue irises in van Gogh's paintings that so inspired me as a child—van Gogh had a profound impact on me and was the earliest influence on how I feel and experience the world through color and texture." Adapted from paintings by Vincent van Gogh. Hooked by Susan Higgins. California. 1997. 23" x 43". *Courtesy of Susan Higgins.*

Detail of "Iris." *Courtesy of Susan Higgins.*

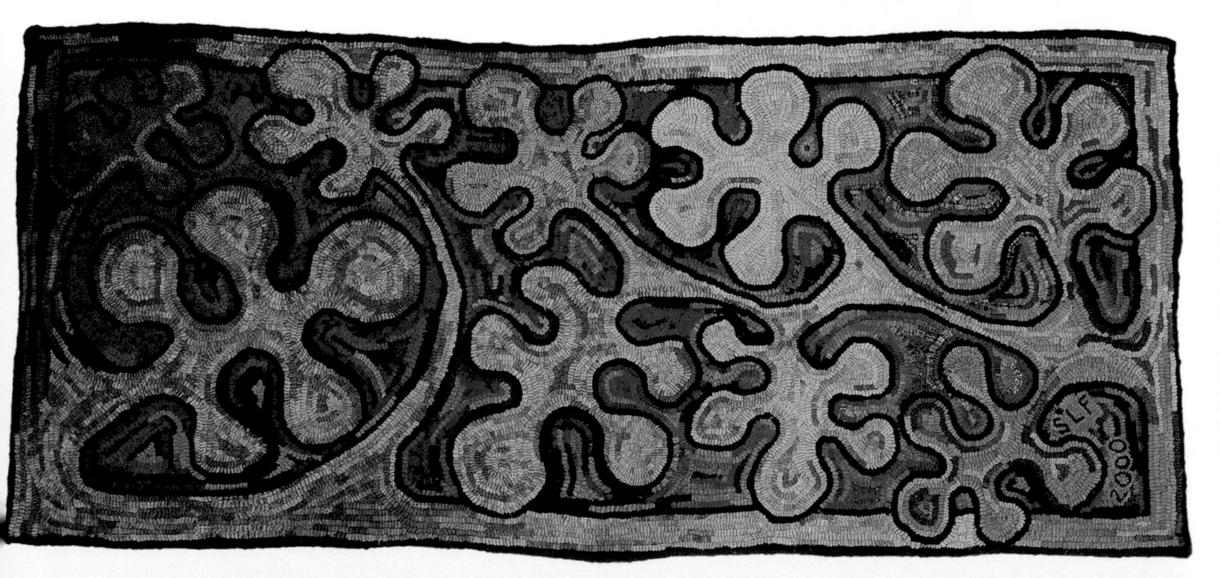

Henri Matisse painted large leaves and Suzan Farrens paid tribute to the impressionist by hooking her own version of his foliage. "Green Leaves." Hooked by Suzan Farrens. California. 2000. 24" x 48." *Courtesy of Suzan Farrens.*

Another Matisse-inspired work. "Blue Leaves." Hooked by Suzan Farrens. California. 2001. 24" x 42". *Courtesy of Suzan Farrens.*

Detail of "Blue Leaves." *Courtesy of Suzan Farrens.*

A hooked tribute to the master of stained glass. "Tiffany Stained Glass Magnolias and Iris." Designed by Jane McGown Flynn. House of Price / Charco pattern. Hooked by Fay Fowler. Missouri. 2004. 32" x 23". *Courtesy of Fay Fowler.*

"Since I am a horse lover, this M. C. Escher design caught my eye when I saw it on the cover of a discarded math text book. All the small spaces made it a challenge to hook, as it was hard to tell which legs went with which horses." "Escher Horses." Adapted from a design by M. C. Escher. Hooked by Gail Majauckas. Massachusetts. 1996. 25" x 32". *Courtesy of Gail Majauckas.*

Hearts and Hooks

The symbol of love, hearts have long graced hooked rugs.

Two hearts take center stage. An eclectic array of abstract and geometric shapes surround the pair. Adapted from a nineteenth century hooked rug—the Barbara Johnson Collection. Hooked On the Creek pattern. Hooked by Davey DeGraff. Vermont. 1999. 34" x 40". *Courtesy of Davey DeGraff.*

Hearts join stars. "This rug hangs in my kitchen, but when I sit in the living room, in my hooking chair, I have it straight in my line of vision. "Kitchen Hearts and Stars." Designed and hooked by Mary Lee O'Connor. New York. 2000. 23" x 23". Courtesy of Mary Lee O'Connor.

Emulating rug makers of days gone by, artist Ann Grover used "what was on hand" to hook this adaptation of an antique rug. "Broken Hearts." Woolley Fox pattern. Hooked by Ann Grover. Texas. 2004. 16" x 30". *Courtesy of Ann Grover.*

Truly a labor of love. Hooked for a first grand-child born in September of 1999. "Heart n' Hand." Quail Hill Designs pattern. Hooked by Tricia Travis. Texas. 1999. 22" x 38". *Courtesy of Tricia Travis*.

Artist Joyce Krueger wanted "a rug full of hearts." Collected heart motifs join those representing the world, the United States, Wisconsin, her church, her husband's place of employment, and rug hooking. "Heart Full of Love." Designed by Joyce Krueger. House of Price / Charco pattern. Hooked by Joyce Krueger. Wisconsin. 2003. 36" x 31". *Courtesy of Joyce Krueger*.

W-I1-T-Bin 60-061794
TJRBAYNE,JESSIE A.(HOOKED ON RUGS)
1/23/2022 3:09:47 PM
061794

Rabbits

Who wouldn't love this floppy eared friend? "Big Bunny with a Big Heart." Designed and hooked by Joyce Connell. Georgia. 2005. 27" x 22". *Courtesy of Joyce Connell.*

Bunnies aren't just for Easter and cartoons anymore. Rug hookers have embraced the long-eared furry creatures and hooked up a hutch full.

Unsuspecting white rabbits play amongst the flowers. A twisted ribbon forms a border around the pair. "Tapestry Bunnies." Designed by Victoria Hart Ingalls. Hooked by JoAn Woody. Missouri. 1998. 25" x 34". *Courtesy of JoAn Woody.*

Standing tall and framed by foliage and flowers. "Harry." Designed by Sally Kallin. Hooked by Alayne Riddle. Missouri. 2004. 29" x 27". *Courtesy of Alayne Riddle.*

Away from troublesome humans and surrounded by a giant "Carrot Patch." Dogwood Hooked Art pattern. Designed and hooked by Chris Lewis. Missouri. 1998. 20" x 26". *Courtesy of Chris Lewis–Dogwood Hooked Art.*

Corner strawberries add touches of color to the leaf-like scrolls that frame Mr. Cottontail. A butterfly diverts the contented rabbit's attention away from the succulent berries. "Bunny's Delight." Designed and hooked by Jean Conrad Johnson. Vermont. 1997. 27" x 36.5". *Courtesy of Jean Conrad Johnson.*

Circle motifs travel from outer borders onto a folk art bunny. "Briar Patch I." Vermont Folk Rugs pattern. Hooked by Polly Reinhart. Pennsylvania. 2001. 24" x 38". *Courtesy of Polly Reinhart.*

"Temptation." Freshly picked produce surrounds two furry friends nestled atop a wooden barrel. "When I saw a picture of this painting I fell in love with it—but my first thought was 'what a challenge!' Because rugs usually take months and years to finish, they generally have a lot of memories attached to them. This rug had a few more than I would have wished for, but it was all worth it." Adapted from a painting by John H. Dill (1830-1888). Hooked by Valerie A. Johnston. North Carolina. 2005. 44" x 28". *Courtesy of Valerie A. Johnston.*

June Mikoryak—
Allen Park, Michigan

Time after time, June Mikoryak's students hook creative, aesthetically pleasing, and award winning rugs. Meticulously crafted from start to finish, rugs hooked under her guidance serve as a benchmark to others in the rug hooking community. Possessing a strong work ethic and blessed with old-world charm, June strives to bring out the best in each student, while always stressing the importance of individuality:

> My interest in rug hooking was generated from a love of art that began at sixteen when I moved from my hometown in rural Illinois to St. Louis, Missouri. I loved the way the "big city" opened doors to interesting places. Visits to the St. Louis Art Museum, where I spent hours admiring the beautiful paintings and sculptures, became a weekly ritual. I moved to Michigan in 1947 and continued to pursue my interests by visiting local museums, historical homes, and plantations, and by taking classes at the Henry Ford Museum and the Detroit Institute of Arts.
>
> In the 1960s, antiques captured my interest and I began collecting that which I admired. All forms of artwork fascinated me. Soon every nook of my home was packed with my new "old" acquisitions. If the local libraries lacked information about my art pieces, I would make appointments with curators from either the Detroit Institute of Arts or the Henry Ford Museum.
>
> I started rug hooking lessons at Greenfield Village in Dearborn in 1974 and have never stopped taking lessons. In 1990, I began teaching rug hooking. The knowledge I gained as an art collector has served me well, and is shared with my students. Often, I refer to an antique oil painting to guide hooking artists with concepts of color, light sources, and shadows.

The mark of a good teacher is seen in the work of his or her students. The following pages offer a sampling of hooked art done by June Mikoryak and many of her talented students.

All rugs were photographed by Michael Reynolds; Michael Reynolds Photography, Plymouth, Michigan.

June Mikoryak's Hooked Art

Hooking artist June Robbs puts her arms around beloved friend, mentor, and rug hooking artist and teacher, June Mikoryak. The two met through a mutual friend in the late 1960s, when June Robbs began buying antiques from the popular dealer who also happened to be named June. When June Mikoryak started teaching rug hooking, June Robbs followed. *Courtesy of June Robbs and Mary von Glahn.*

Blossoming poppies, buds, and feathery foliage welcome all—a decorating plus for any home. "The Glad Hand." Designed by Pearl McGown. W. Cushing and Company pattern. Hooked by June Mikoryak. Michigan. 2005. 28.5" x 43". *Courtesy of June Mikoryak.*

Hooked with love. "For Your Love." Lavish scrolls complement a lush oval floral medallion. Designed by Jane McGown Flynn. House of Price / Charco pattern. Hooked by June Mikoryak. Michigan. 2004. 32" x 50". *Courtesy of June Mikoryak.*

This Persian-style rug, hooked in a harmonious palette, speaks of a proud Iranian heritage. "Riza." Designed by Pearl McGown. W. Cushing and Company pattern. Hooked by June Mikoryak. Michigan. 2003. 36" x 60". *Courtesy of June Mikoryak.*

Inspired by a century old hooked rug, "Geometric Star" is a design that defies time and appeals to a wide audience. The interaction of light and dark colors is reminiscent of a stained glass window. New Earth Designs pattern. Hooked by June Mikoryak. Michigan. 2002. 28" x 40". *Courtesy of June Mikoryak.*

A challenging project magnificently executed. Named for the ancient Persian poet and astronomer, "Omar Khayyám." Designed by Pearl McGown. W. Cushing and Company pattern. Hooked by June Mikoryak. Michigan. 2005. 84" x 60". *Courtesy of June Mikoryak.*

"Masterful Morris." Concentric linear borders frame free flowing scroll-like leaves and stylized flowers. Modeled after the work of English artist, poet, and socialist William Morris (1834-1896). Designed by Jane McGown Flynn. House of Price / Charco pattern. Hooked by June Mikoryak. Michigan. 1996. 18" x 26". *Courtesy of June Mikoryak.*

Ripe and ready to eat. A banner of delectable fruit. "Delicious Dozen." Designed by Jane McGown Flynn. House of Price / Charco pattern. Hooked by June Mikoryak. Michigan. 1997. 11.5" x 45". *Courtesy of June Mikoryak.*

Right:
"Silken Sunburst." Floral and decorative motifs, hooked in subtle tones, combine in a pleasing mirror image pattern. Designed by Jane McGown Flynn. House of Price / Charco pattern. Hooked by June Mikoryak. Michigan. 1999. 11" x 22". *Courtesy of June Mikoryak.*

Hooked Art—Under the Guidance of June Mikoryak

Fun and cheerful and much like the artist that hooked "Pam's Geometric." Shapes and colors merge and blend. Designed and hooked by Pam Alexander. Michigan. 2005. 20" x 28". *Courtesy of Pam Alexander.*

The best of both worlds. "Originally this was to be a folk art chicken. When drawing the front half, it looked like a hen, while the back half has the feathers of a rooster." A chicken wire fence provides a patterned backdrop for "La Solitaire Poulet." Designed and hooked by Doreen E. Bollinger. Michigan. 2005. 28" x 43". *Courtesy of Doreen E. Bollinger.*

Delicate fanciful flowers and vines intermingle to form "Willow Bank." An exceptional hooked interpretation of crewel embroidery. Designed by Jane McGown Flynn. House of Price / Charco pattern. Hooked by Paula Brannon. Michigan. 2005. 34" x 52". *Courtesy of Paula Brannon.*

Paula Brannon hooked "Antique Charm" as gift for her parents to commemorate their 50th wedding anniversary. An angular border of Southwestern influence contains blossoms, large and small. Designed by Jane McGown Flynn. House of Price / Charco pattern. Hooked by Paula Brannon. Michigan. 1996. 28" x 43". *Courtesy of Paula Brannon.*

"Gentle Giant," a parading pachyderm complete with tasseled finery. Rose panels and stylized floral borders of an Indian persuasion enhance the hooked portrait. Designed by Jane McGown Flynn. House of Price / Charco pattern. Hooked by Janet M. Burg. Michigan. 2000. 30" x 51". *Courtesy of Janet M. Burg.*

Twin images of noblemen atop elephants, accompanied by huntsmen, horsemen, dogs, birds, and flying carpets, recall tales of ancient India. "Kashani Hunt." Designed by Jane McGown Flynn. House of Price / Charco pattern. Hooked by Janet M. Burg. Michigan. 2000. 72" x 43". *Courtesy of Janet M. Burg.*

An updated design and spark of color brings new life to a favorite quilt pattern turned rug pattern. "Log Cabin Repeat Revised." Designed by Jane McGown Flynn. House of Price / Charco pattern. Hooked by Janet M. Burg. Michigan. 2003. 24" x 33". *Courtesy of Janet M. Burg.*

At home, relaxed and creating a patriotic rug. "Hooking Sweet Hooking." A light-hearted look at a whimsical character. Beverly Conway Designs pattern. Hooked by Janet M. Burg. Michigan. 2004. 34" x 28". *Courtesy of Janet M. Burg.*

Pennsylvania Dutch inspired floral sprays fill a bright and cheerful oval. "Sweet Sue." Designed by Chris Parker. Hooked by Janet M. Burg. Michigan. 2005. 26" x 37". *Courtesy of Janet M. Burg.*

Bold and graphic. "Compass." Golden rays lead the way. Quail Hill Designs pattern. Hooked by Jean Byrd. Michigan.1999. Diameter 48". *Courtesy of Jean Byrd.*

A pleasing combination of diamond and floral motifs. Adapted from an antique rug. Hooked by Jean Byrd. Michigan. 2001. 31" x 48". *Courtesy of Jean Byrd.*

"Wingford Farm." Artist Terry Campbell fashioned a unique collage of that which is near and dear. Designed and hooked by Terry Campbell. Michigan. 2004. 32" x 54". *Courtesy of Terry Campbell.*

An eagle envelopes a leisurely moment on and off the water at the aforementioned "Wingford Farm." Leaves turn to stars enriching a patriotic theme. "Love Many Trust Few." Designed by Pris Buttler. Hooked by Terry Campbell. Michigan. 2004. 40" x 34". *Courtesy of Terry Campbell.*

Angular and scrolled borders circumscribe a stately stag poised in a vintage frame. Adapted from an E. S. Frost pattern. Hooked by Terry Campbell. Michigan. 2005. 26" x 36". *Courtesy of Terry Campbell.*

A contented Chesapeake Bay retriever dreams of favorite things. "Clark's Parker 'Day'." Designed by Brock Clark. Hooked by Brenda Clark. Michigan. 2003. 29" x 48". *Courtesy of Brenda Clark of Old Orchard Primitives.*

Brenda Clark captures the daily activities at the "Clark Homestead." Designed by Brenda Clark and Pris Buttler. Hooked by Brenda Clark. Michigan. 2003. 37" x 48". *Courtesy of Brenda Clark of Old Orchard Primitives.*

Colors, not often found in Oriental rugs, lend themselves to this unique and aesthetically pleasing rug. The background was hooked in a horizontal direction to mimic its hand-woven counterpart. Adapted from an Oriental rug. Hooked by Brenda Clark. Michigan. 2005. 30" x 54". *Courtesy of Brenda Clark of Old Orchard Primitives.*

Primitive roses, buds, and leaves recall hooked rugs of the late 1800s. "Old Floral." Woolley Fox pattern. Hooked by Brenda Clark. Michigan. 2004. 32" x 57". *Courtesy of Brenda Clark of Old Orchard Primitives.*

Recalling motifs found on an antique "Ohio Coverlet." A nearly symmetrical design is interrupted by the loving gaze of feathered fowl. Stylized berries on a scalloped vine frame the pair. Adapted from an Edyth O'Neill design. Woolley Fox pattern. Hooked by Brenda Clark. Michigan. 2005. 27" x 41.5". *Courtesy of Brenda Clark of Old Orchard Primitives.*

A rug to delight any child. Two teddy bears enjoy a spin around the May pole. "Escape." Designed and hooked by Dee Doria. Michigan. 2002. 26" x 40". *Courtesy of Dee Doria.*

Dee Doria, depicted as a child, romps in the leaves with the dog she never had but always wanted. The shape of the rug is a stylized Black Jack oak leaf. "Fall Fantasy." Designed and hooked by Dee Doria. Michigan. 2003. 38" x 28". *Courtesy of Dee Doria.*

"Beary Scary." Frightened of butterflies? Out of the forest darkness and into the light. Designed and hooked by Dee Doria. Michigan. 2004. 28" x 42". *Courtesy of Dee Doria*.

Rug makers, housebound by harsh winter weather, do get a lot of hooking done but often wish, like this scarecrow, "If only I could get loose and fly south." "Jivin' Scarecrow." Designed and hooked by Dee Doria. Michigan. 2004. 38" x 28". *Courtesy of Dee Doria*.

A stained glass window highlights the face of one who contemplates the world. Fashioned in an Art Nouveau manner. "Serenity." Designed and hooked by Dee Doria. Michigan. 2004. 46" x 27". *Courtesy of Dee Doria*.

"Inquisitorial." Hooking artist Dee Doria offers a glimpse of a quilt maker inspecting her work from a unique vantage point; through a wooden porch structure. Note the window-like shape of the rug. Designed and hooked by Dee Doria. Michigan. 2004. 34" x 45". *Courtesy of Dee Doria*.

Kaleidoscope colors radiate out from a vivid green pom-pom center. This bold and bright geometric design rug boasts a hexagonal shape. "Nova." Designed and hooked by Dee Doria. Michigan. 2005. 43" x 48". *Courtesy of Dee Doria.*

Rug hookers are always looking for ways to use up leftovers from other projects. "Scraps" were used to fashion this lively trio of stars. Designed by Jane McGown Flynn. House of Price / Charco pattern. Hooked by Dee Doria. Michigan. 2004. 24" x 36". *Courtesy of Dee Doria.*

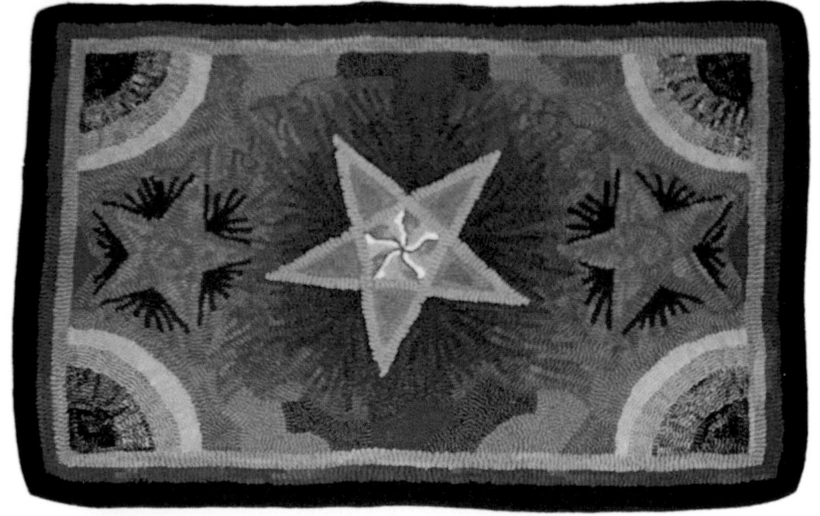

Thistles and sheep recalled memories of "Scotland My Scotland." A salt marsh caterpillar savors a succulent leaf in the lower right hand corner. Quail Hill Designs pattern. Hooked by Dee Doria. Michigan. 2001. 34" x 46". *Courtesy of Dee Doria.*

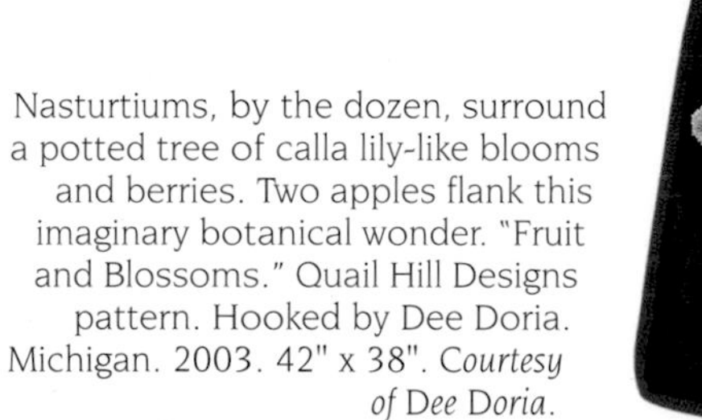

Nasturtiums, by the dozen, surround a potted tree of calla lily-like blooms and berries. Two apples flank this imaginary botanical wonder. "Fruit and Blossoms." Quail Hill Designs pattern. Hooked by Dee Doria. Michigan. 2003. 42" x 38". *Courtesy of Dee Doria.*

A curious cat finds himself in a garden of herbs and written word. "The Herb Rug." Quail Hill Designs pattern. Hooked by Dee Doria. Michigan. 2003. 72" x 36". *Courtesy of Dee Doria.*

An oval portraiture of two sheep rests on a field of floral sprays. Hooked with strips of woolen fabric and yarns. "Sheep Festival." Quail Hill Designs pattern. Hooked by Dee Doria. Michigan. 2002. 37" x 69". *Courtesy of Dee Doria.*

Eight blocks, in each a different flower. Four birds, of varying species, complete the "Songbird Quilt." Quail Hill Designs pattern. Hooked by Dee Doria. Michigan. 2004. 37" x 69". *Courtesy of Dee Doria.*

Decorating a winter landscape with "Hanging Stars." Dee Doria created this rug as a tribute to her three daughters and used a combination of solid, tweed, and plaid woolen fabrics to hook the playful angels. Designed by Pris Buttler. Hooked by Dee Doria. Michigan. 2003. 20" x 44". *Courtesy of Dee Doria.*

"Ally's Cat," complete with sparse electrified fur, was adapted from a drawing done by a five-year-old granddaughter. Designed by Alaina Siler. Hooked by Cindi Gay. Ohio. 2004. 34.5" x 51". *Courtesy of Cindi Gay.*

A hooked glimpse into the past. Mottled pastel shades create a backdrop for the "General." Adapted from a recent photo of David Gay (the artist's husband) dressed in a vintage Civil War uniform. Hooked by Cindi Gay. Ohio. 2004. 21" x 16". *Courtesy of Cindi Gay.*

Primitive flowered vines burst forth in a pleasing palette. "Sailcloth." Heirloom Rug pattern. Hooked by Marie Johnson. Michigan. 1995. 30" x 70". *Courtesy of Marie Johnson.*

No matter where you roam, there's "No Place Like Home." Hearts and heart-shaped buds decorate the ideal house. Designed by Laurice Heath. Hooked by Marie Johnson. Michigan. 2000. 24" x 36". *Courtesy of Marie Johnson.*

Vibrant touches of gold and blue add jewel-like tones to a favorite pattern. "Cape Cod Runner." Harry M. Fraser Company pattern. Hooked by Dan Kirk. Michigan. 2001. 27" x 92". *Courtesy of Dan Kirk.*

A rug to delight both young and old. "Bug and Vine." Winged and crawling creatures visit imaginary flowers. DiFranza Designs pattern. Hooked by Dan Kirk. Michigan. 2004. 30" x 40". *Courtesy of Dan Kirk.*

Fond sentiments frame "Nanna's House." A beloved home proudly displays the American flag. Designed and hooked by Nancy Klemmer. Michigan. 2002. 27" x 32". *Courtesy of Nancy Klemmer.*

Delicate twigs emerge from an elaborate S curve swag. A mottled neutral background enhances the scroll study. "Nordic Fest." Designed by Jane McGown Flynn. House of Price / Charco pattern. Hooked by Karen L. Krepps. Michigan. 2005. 16" x 31". *Courtesy of Karen L. Krepps.*

Is this a photograph? True to life "Spring Iris" reach across a rich, dark field. Designed by Jane McGown Flynn. House of Price / Charco pattern. Hooked by Karen L. Krepps. Michigan. 2005. 26" x 44". *Courtesy of Karen L. Krepps.*

A central diamond medallion anchors a matching pair of multi-flowered stalks. Adapted from an old tombstone motif. "Stone Flowers." Designed and hooked by Karen L. Krepps. Michigan. 2003. 48" x 45". *Courtesy of Karen L. Krepps.*

Holding on to a prize morsel. A handsome marbleized background and ebony frame, complete with prints, complement this hooked "Crow." Designed and hooked by Karen L. Krepps. Michigan. 1999. 34" x 45". *Courtesy of Karen L. Krepps.*

Pictured is the Bradley homestead in Sparta, Tennessee, the artist's great-grandparent's home. Grandfather Paul Bradley feeds a flock of baby chicks. "Granny's Rug." Designed and hooked by Karen L. Krepps. Michigan. 2002. 33" x 40". *Courtesy of Karen L. Krepps.*

"Nice and Easy." A stylized bouquet, hooked in shades of purple and pink, is protected by a dentil border. Designed by Jane McGown Flynn. House of Price/ Charco pattern. Hooked by Beverly Lynch. Michigan. 2003. 20" x 34". *Courtesy of Beverly Lynch.*

A crescent moon lights the way for a white-tailed deer frolicking in the snow "Up North." Acorns and a fishing lure frame the postcard image of "the best place to be." Designed and hooked by Laura Milliken. Michigan. 2003. 20" x 36". *Courtesy of Laura Milliken.*

"Oak Scrollings," a resplendent, finely shaded leaf and acorn composition, is reminiscent of an ornate antique gilt frame. Designed by Jane McGown Flynn. House of Price / Charco pattern. Hooked by Laura L. Milliken. Michigan. 2002. 21" x 32". *Courtesy of Laura L. Milliken.*

Leaflets join forces with stylized diamonds to create a pleasing optical illusion. "Hickory Leaves." Harry M. Fraser Company pattern. Hooked by Laura L. Milliken. Michigan. 2005. 27" x 36.5". *Courtesy of Laura L. Milliken.*

Sunflowers dance around a rooster-topped weathervane. The colors used within are repeated in the outer border. "Sunflower Rooster." Designed by Diane Kelly. Hooked by Chris Needels. Michigan. 2002. 38" x 54". *Courtesy of Chris Needels.*

Primitive flowers hooked in a lively manner. "Sailcloth." Heirloom Rug pattern. Hooked by Chris Needels. Michigan. 2002. 30" x 70". *Courtesy of Chris Needels.*

A colorful floral medallion fills a rich blue field. "Little Win." Designed by Pearl McGown. W. Cushing and Company pattern. Hooked by Francesca Payne. Michigan. 2003. 30" x 44". *Courtesy of Francesca Payne.*

Reminiscent of a Victorian calling card. Delicate pastel blossoms and lace-like details recall another era. "Rose Point." Designed by Pearl McGown. W. Cushing and Company pattern. Hooked by Denise Pentiak. Michigan. 1999. 29" x 45". *Courtesy of Denise Pentiak.*

Stylized peacocks flank a decorative handled urn. Curlicue stems support a creative blend of fantasy flowers and foliage. "Garden Enchantment." Designed and hooked by Denise Pentiak. Michigan. 2001. 46" x 74". *Courtesy Denise Pentiak.*

"Grand Daddy Smith and His Bear." "My grandfather, George Smith, accompanied by his trained bear, operated a small ferry boat that traveled between Michigan's Lake Charlevoix and Round Lake. The *Minnie*, named after my grandmother, ferried tourists between the downtown areas, resort hotels, and the depot." Pictured is the *Minnie* as she passes the Belvedere Hotel. Designed and hooked by Cynthia L. Postmus. Michigan. 2005. 22" x 29". *Courtesy of Cynthia L. Postmus.*

Jewel-like tones enhance hooked symbols of hospitality. "Pineapple Antique." Quail Hill Designs pattern. Hooked by June Robbs. Michigan. 1997. 36" x 72". *Courtesy of June Robbs.*

Dressed in their finest and the envy of all. "Easter Parade." "A memorial rug for my mother who always made sure her girls looked grand on Easter." Artist June Robbs recalls fond memories with her hook and strips of woolen fabric. Adapted from a turn of the century postcard. Hooked by June Robbs. Michigan. 2005. 32" x 39.5". *Courtesy of June Robbs.*

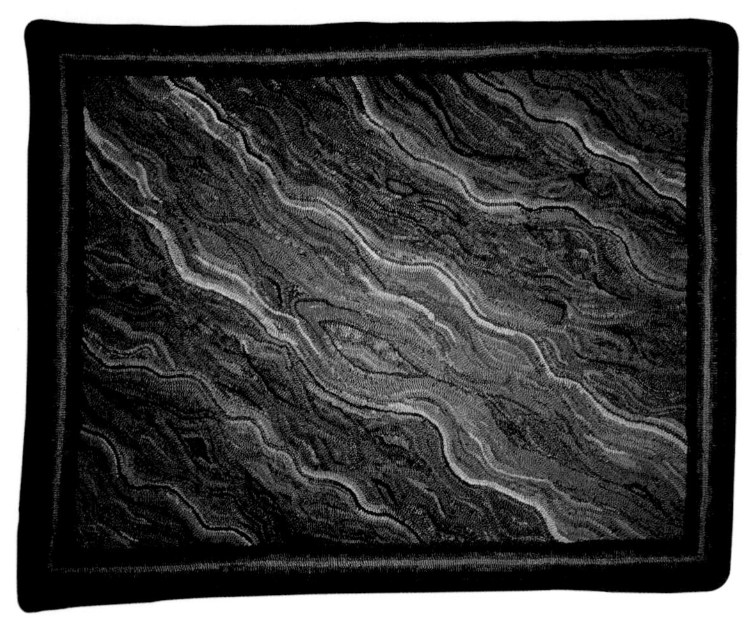

"Northern Exposure." Earth, tree bark, shoreline, and more. A harmonious compilation of nature's best portrayed in an abstract manner. Designed and hooked by June Robbs. Michigan. 2002. 36" x 44". *Courtesy of June Robbs.*

"This is my big and fat female orange cat, 'Annie Belle,' who is still with us and is still fat and much loved." Designed by Pearl McGown. W. Cushing and Company pattern. Hooked by June Robbs. Michigan. 1999. Diameter 15". *Courtesy of June Robbs.*

Ornamental flowers, foliage, and Massachusetts' native berry, the cranberry, are vivid against a rich dark field. "Cape Cod." Harry M. Fraser Company pattern. Hooked by June Robbs. Michigan. 1997. 32" x 36". *Courtesy of June Robbs.*

"Betty." A feline fantasy feast. Adapted, with permission, from designer Mimi Vang Olsen's original art work "Bushy." Hooked by June Robbs. Michigan. 2003. 41" x 49.5". *Courtesy of June Robbs.*

Bold waves of color merge. "Memorial to my father, John Middleton, a true 'free spirit.'" "John's Carpet." Adapted from an antique rug. Hooked by June Robbs. Michigan. 2004. 30" x 48.5". *Courtesy of June Robbs.*

"Pomegranates." Large tart berries upon which to sit. Quail Hill Designs pattern. Hooked by June Robbs. Michigan. 2005. 18" x 18". *Courtesy of June Robbs.*

"Checks and Arrows," a striking geometric design. June Robbs takes control and masters a select palette. Adapted from an antique rug pattern. Hooked by June Robbs. Michigan. 2005. 57" x 35". *Courtesy of June Robbs.*

Peace and serenity can be found by a "Mountain Stream." Designed by Jane McGown Flynn. House of Price / Charco pattern. Hooked by Mary Sawyer. Michigan. 2004. 23" x 19". *Courtesy of Mary Sawyer.*

Inspired by the delicate motifs found on china. Three lush roses grace the center of "Wedgwood." Designed by Pearl McGown. W. Cushing and Company pattern. Hooked by Mary Sawyer. Michigan. 2001. 34.5" x 42.5". *Courtesy of Mary Sawyer.*

Below:
Up and away we go, soaring above fields and farms. Choosing a unique sky color complements not only the airborne pair, but also the landscape below. "Flying Hare." Designed by Jane Gassner for Primco. Hooked by Cheryl Singley. Michigan 2001. 32" x 34". *Courtesy of Cheryl Singley.*

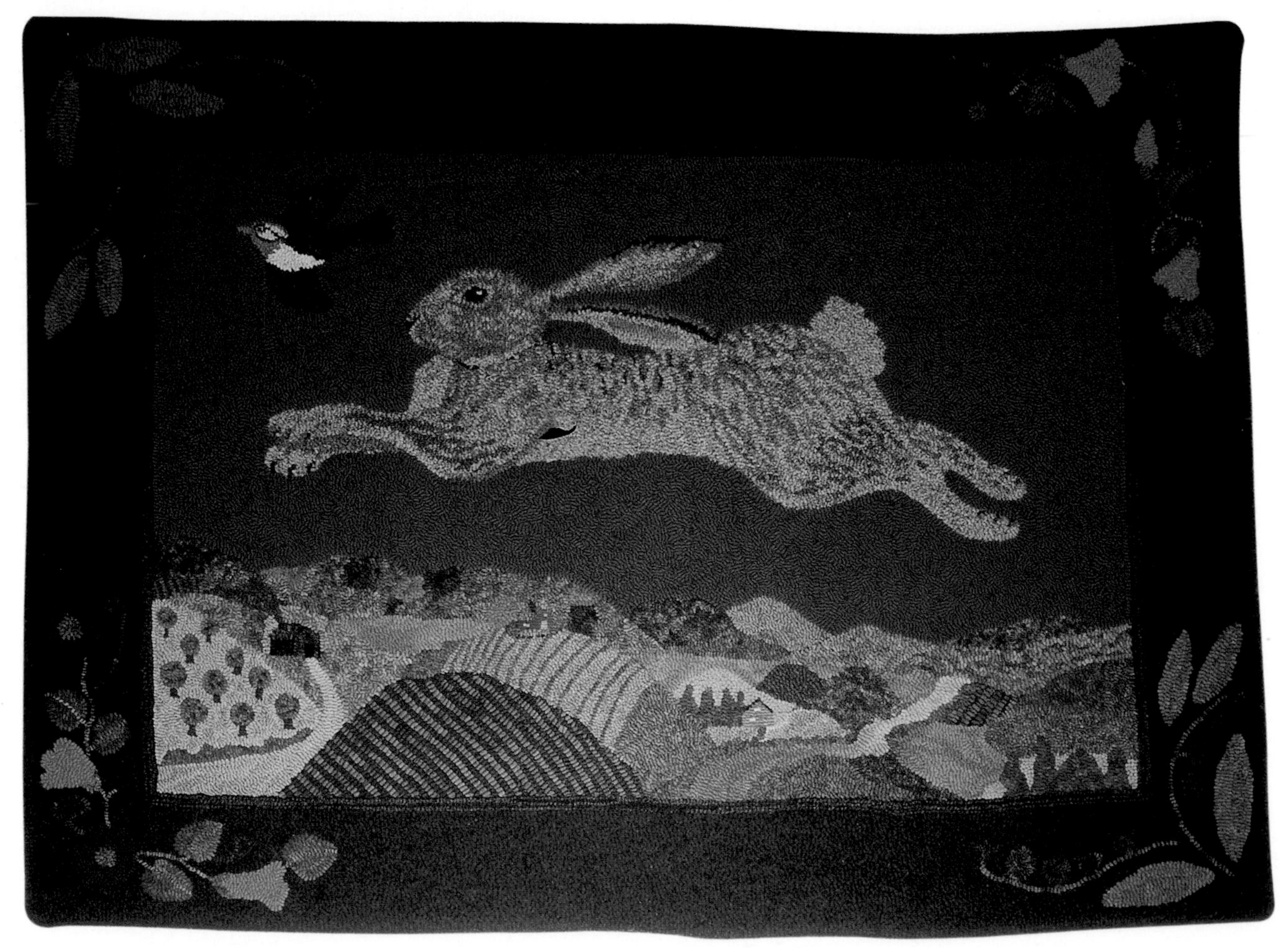

Recalling carved wood and architectural elements. "Guilfor Runner." Designed by Edyth O'Neill. Woolley Fox pattern. Hooked by Cheryl Singley. Michigan. 2004. 14" x 31". *Courtesy of Cheryl. Singley.*

The glory that is autumn forms a "Rustic Wreath." Attention was paid to the smallest of details so that every hooked leaf, pine bough, pinecone, acorn, and berry appears life-like. Designed by Jane McGown Flynn. House of Price / Charco pattern. Hooked by Cheryl Singley. Michigan 1995. 26" x 36". *Courtesy of Cheryl Singley.*

Right:
Another interpretation of a favorite pattern using a pink and blue color scheme. "Nice and Easy." Designed by Jane McGown Flynn. House of Price / Charco pattern. Hooked by Cheryl Singley. Michigan. 1999. 38" x 72". *Courtesy of Cheryl Singley.*

Modern rug hookers and pattern makers embrace the needlework first done in the seventeenth century during the reign of Queen Elizabeth I. Crewel-like vines, laden with fanciful flowers, foliage, and fruit, form the traditional and popular pattern, "Queen Mary." Designed by Pearl McGown. W. Cushing and Company pattern. Hooked by Cheryl Singley. Michigan. 1999. 38" x 72". *Courtesy of Cheryl Singley.*

"Shaker Tree of Life" was intended to be a future wedding gift for Bradley Storck's young daughter, Mollie. Unfortunately, her life was cut short by illness. With the rug hooked at her hospital bedside, Mollie lost her courageous battle shortly after her second birthday. Designed by Pearl McGown. W. Cushing and Company pattern. Hooked by Bradley D. Storck. Michigan. 1999. 33" x 45". *Courtesy of Bradley D. Storck.*

Inspired by his son Bradley's hooking and how it helped him get through the pain of losing his daughter Mollie, grandfather Donald Storck picked up a hook and created "Sheep Rug." DiFranza Designs pattern. Hooked by Donald T. Storck. Michigan. 2003. 24" x 36". *Courtesy of Donald T. Storck.*

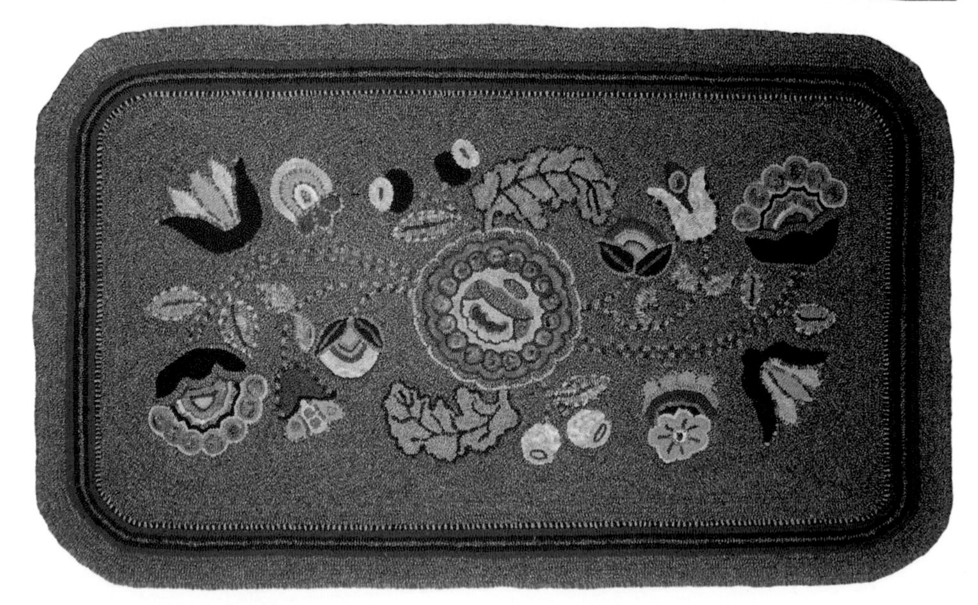

Ethel Storck, wife of Donald and mother of Bradley, also wanted to try her hand at rug hooking. She created "1852 Antique Rug." Stylized floral sprays radiate out from a central flower-like medallion. DiFranza Designs pattern. Hooked by Ethel P. Storck. Michigan. 2003. 28" x 48". *Courtesy of Ethel P. Storck.*

A yellow blossom takes center stage. Another interpretation of a popular pattern. "Nice and Easy." Designed by Jane McGown Flynn. House of Price / Charco pattern. Hooked by Ethel P. Storck. Michigan 2005. 20" x 34". *Courtesy of Ethel P. Storck.*

"Tom 2." A fine feathered turkey. Feather-shaped motifs enhance a simple border frame. Designed by Emma Lou Lais. Hooked by Ethel P. Storck. Michigan. 2005. 27.5 x 24". *Courtesy of Ethel P. Storck.*

Grand and glorious "Queen Mary." Hooked crewel work at its best. Designed by Pearl McGown. W. Cushing and Company pattern. Hooked by Irena Wrona. Michigan. 2000. 38" x 72". *Courtesy of Irena Wrona.*

Finely shaded scrolls frame "Springtime," an artistic arrangement of early flowers and foliage. Designed by Anita Allen. W. Cushing and Company pattern. Hooked by Irena Wrona. Michigan. 1999. 28.5" x 46". *Courtesy of Irena Wrona.*

A hooked children's nursery rhyme takes on a painterly quality. "Mary's Lamb." Adapted from a circa 1916 Blanche Wright illustration. Hooked by Irena Wrona. Michigan. 2002. 30" x 32". *Courtesy of Irena Wrona.*

The "Ducks" take a stroll. Adapted from an E. S. Frost pattern. Hooked by Irena Wrona. Michigan. 1997. 17" x 35.5". *Courtesy of Irena Wrona.*

A Hooked Place to Rest Your Weary Feet

What better place to rest your weary feet than on something hooked. Rug makers are truly an ingenious and industrious lot.

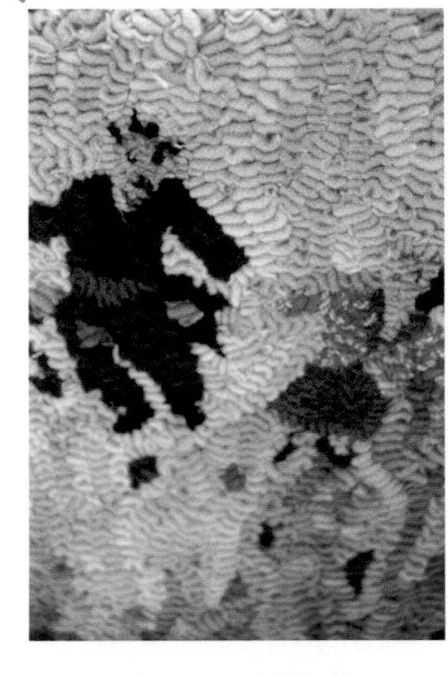

This detail from the back side of the "Wedding Rocker" pictures the father of the bride with money spilling from his pockets. *Courtesy of Kim Nixon.*

Detail of the front side of the "Wedding Rocker" depicts "the bride going forth into the other world. She leads the way dangling her husband behind—who holds his mother-in-law's hand." *Courtesy of Kim Nixon.*

"Wedding Rocker." The journey into marital bliss. Seat and back designed and hooked by Kim Nixon. Tennessee. 2004. 17.5" w x 32.5" l x 30" ht. *Courtesy of Kim Nixon.*

"Snake Stool." Autumn colored leaves cannot conceal this bold and bright-skinned reptile. Designed and hooked by Kim Nixon. Tennessee. 2003. 10" w x 15.5" l x 14" ht. *Courtesy of Kim Nixon.*

"Peace Dove Stool." Inspired by the Hopi saying, "The swiftest thing to fly is the mind. Those who know this have wings." Designed and hooked by Kim Nixon. Tennessee. 2003. 10" w x 15.5" l x 14" ht. *Courtesy of Kim Nixon.*

Detail of "Snake Stool." Slithering through fall foliage. *Courtesy of Kim Nixon.*

Eve feeds the serpent. "Adam and Eve Stool." Designed and hooked by Kim Nixon. Tennessee. 2003. 13" w x 13" l x 16.5" ht. *Courtesy of Kim Nixon.*

"Teacup Stool." Put your feet up and have a cup of tea. Designed and hooked by Kim Nixon. Tennessee. 2003. 11" w x 16" l x 10" ht. *Courtesy of Kim Nixon.*

"Iris Cube." A diamond-patterned backdrop highlights spring flowers. Designed and hooked by Kim Nixon. Tennessee. 2004. 13" w x 13" l x 16.5" ht. *Courtesy of Kim Nixon.*

"Flying Angel Stool." A free spirit soars in sunny skies. Designed and hooked by Kim Nixon. Tennessee. 2004. 10" w x 14" l x 10" ht. *Courtesy of Kim Nixon.*

"Garden Bench." A hooked postcard image. Designed and hooked by Kim Nixon. Tennessee. 2004. 11.5" w x 25.5" l x 24" ht. *Courtesy of Kim Nixon.*

"Goddess Stool." A comforting invitation to rest your royal feet. Designed and hooked by Kim Nixon. Tennessee. 2003. 14" w x 14" l x 12" ht. *Courtesy of* Kim Nixon.

"Seasons." A decorating must-have for spring, summer, fall, and winter. Designed and hooked by Kim Nixon. Tennessee. 2003. 13" w x 13" l x 16.5" ht. *Courtesy of* Kim Nixon.

Detail of "Goddess Stool." *Courtesy of* Kim Nixon.

An interlocking pattern covers a "Geometric Bench." Designed and hooked by Kim Nixon. Tennessee. 2004. 11" w x 25.5" l x 24" ht. *Courtesy of* Kim Nixon.

Hooked on the Sea

Hooking lore tells of seafaring men fashioning rugs while aboard whaling ships in the mid 1800s. Over a century and a half later, hooking rugs with nautical themes remains popular with modern fiber artists.

Drawing upon her love for boats and travel posters plus a collection of nautical images, Ruth Hennessey fashioned "Sailors and Ships." Hooked ocean currents form a backdrop for the sea-related collage. Designed and hooked by Ruth Hennessy. New York. 2004. 33" x 44". *Courtesy of Ruth Hennessey.*

A vigilant watch pays off. "Our Captain Stood Upon the Deck." Pris Buttler Rug Designs pattern. Hooked by Lee Abrego. Maine 2002. 27" x 46". *Courtesy of Lee Abrego.*

"Schooner." With no factual image available, Edyth O'Neill fabricated a representation of what she believed the six-gun Connecticut ship "Spy" would have looked like. A banner of stars represents the original thirteen colonies. Designed by Edyth O'Neill. Woolley Fox pattern. Hooked by Edyth O'Neill. Texas. 2003. 36" x 46". *Courtesy of Edyth O'Neill.*

Stern at the wheel but gentle with "The Captain's Cats." Inspired by a drawing by Feodor Rojankovsky and the first four lines of a poem by Elizabeth Coatsworth. From the 1943 A *Giant Golden Book—Dogs, Cats and Horses—61 Stories and Poems*. Dogwood Hooked Art pattern. Hooked by Ariel Baker. Missouri. 1998. 36" x 60". *Courtesy of Ariel Baker–Dogwood Hooked Art.*

This rug pays tribute to Robert Nordberg, a sea-going great-grandfather who sailed around the world seven times. In his spare moments, he built ship models, shadow boxes, and carved low relief nautical scenes. His small carved image of a ship under sail inspired artist Victoria Hart Ingalls, the great-granddaughter he never knew, to hook "Papa's Ship." Designed and hooked by Victoria Hart Ingalls. Missouri. 2004. 11" x 15". *Courtesy of Victoria Hart Ingalls.*

Edyth O'Neill created the pattern for "Oliver Cromwell" after viewing ship models at the Maritime Museum in Essex, Connecticut. Note the inclusion of a whale in the fanciful wave-like border. Designed by Edyth O'Neill. Woolley Fox pattern. Hooked by Edyth O'Neill. Texas. 1997. 37" x 49". *Courtesy of Edyth O'Neill.*

Inspired by an antique painting, hooking artist Beverly Osgood complemented "The General Brown" with an original border of shell, rope, and quarter board motifs. Shades of blue were hooked to mimic the ocean's movement and to create the illusion of grain painting. Designed and hooked by Beverly Osgood. Connecticut. 2003. 30" x 53". *Courtesy of Beverly Osgood.*

Another rug hooker's interpretation of the "Oliver Cromwell" pattern. White sails and a colorful border are intensified by a rich dark background. Designed by Edyth O'Neill. Woolley Fox pattern. Hooked by Barbara Bentley. Texas. 2004. 37" x 49". *Courtesy of Barbara Bentley.*

One gold star breaks the patriot palette used to portray the *Liberty* under sail on a moonlit night. "Liberty Ship." Designed by Renee Nanneman–The Need'L Love Company. Hooked by Barbara Ahlbrand. Illinois. 2001. 30" x 30". *Courtesy of Barbara Ahlbrand.*

Judith Dallegret's great-grandfathers, sea captains all, left their home port of Sandy Cove, Nova Scotia and sailed around the globe. "Storms at Sea," hooked in their memory, was made for the artist's Bay of Fundy home. Designed and hooked by Judith Dallegret. Quebec, Canada. 2001. 28" x 48". *Courtesy of Judith Dallegret.*

A "Mariner's Compass" helped to guide sailors through uncharted waters. Adapted from a photograph of an antique rug. Hooked by Nancy L. Brown. New Hampshire. 2002. 34.5" x 34.5". *Courtesy of Nancy L. Brown.*

Scenic "Peggy's Cove, Nova Scotia" was photographed, painted, and hooked by artist Kathleen VanLoozen. Oregon. 2002. 39.5" x 24.5". *Courtesy of Kathleen VanLoozen.*

Northern lights dance behind a guiding "Lighthouse." Linda Smith's very successful first attempt at rug hooking combines bold planes of solid vibrant color with the softness of hooked tweeds and plaids. Deanna Fitzpatrick pattern. Hooked by Linda L. Smith. Vermont. 2004. 24" x 12". *Courtesy of Linda L. Smith.*

One of Maine's most scenic views portrayed in miniature dimensions. "Portland Lighthouse." Jacqueline Designs pattern. Hooked by Shirley S. Lothrop. Maine. 2004. 10" x 17". *Courtesy of Shirley S. Lothrop.*

"'I Spy' both land and sea," says he who stands watch porch side. Pris Buttler Designs pattern. Hooked by Judy Howarth. Maine. 2005. 28" x 29". *Courtesy of Judy Howarth.*

Capturing all that is Maine. Rugged seacoast, lighthouse, and clipper ship are framed with shells, shore roses, and rope. The colorful border was fashioned in the Waldoboro-style of raising, clipping, and sculpturing the hooked loops. "Maine Coast Scenic." Jacqueline Designs pattern. Designed and hooked by Jacqueline Hansen. Maine. 1998. 32" x 38". *Courtesy of Jacqueline Hansen.*

The sun sets and the moon rises as the *Champagne* sails past Southeast Light on Rhode Island's Block Island. Diane Yudin recalls thirty years of wonderful memories spent with her husband aboard their 42' sloop. "Champagne Sail." Designed and hooked by Diane Yudin. Connecticut. 1996. 80" x 40". *Courtesy of Diane Yudin.*

Detail of "Champagne Sail." *Courtesy of Diane Yudin.*

Choppy waves and steady winds move along "Ships at Sea." Note the artist's initials in the smoke rising from the house on the ledge. Designed and hooked by Susie Stephenson. Maine. 2005. 21" x 28". *Courtesy of Susie Stephenson.*

Paying homage to the earth, sea, and sky. Cresting, wave-like curlicues frame "East Rock." Designed and hooked by Judy Fresk. Connecticut. 2001. 40" x 33". *Courtesy of Judy Fresk.*

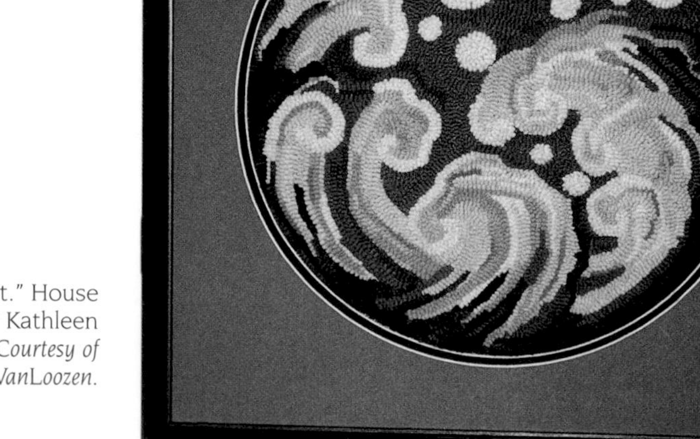

Frothy foam churns on turbulent waters. "Crest." House of Price / Charco pattern. Hooked by Kathleen VanLoozen. Oregon. 2004. Diameter 14". *Courtesy of Kathleen VanLoozen.*

Riding Bahamian-colored waves, a mermaid plays with a fish trio. Coral and seaweed intertwine and border the undulating shaped rug. "The Wave." Designed and hooked by Diane Yudin. Connecticut. 1998. 60" x 50". *Courtesy of Diane Yudin.*

A beguiling hooked lady of the sea is adorned with hand-dyed silk, hand-spun yarns, beads, pearls, and shells. "Heather's Mermaid." Designed and hooked by Heather Ritchie. Yorkshire, England. 2002. 60" x 50". *Courtesy of Private Collection.*

"Mermaids At Sea." A blonde, brunette, and redhead frolic in the ocean waves. The salty threesome portray the artist's water-loving daughters. Designed and hooked by Beverly Goodrich. Georgia. 2002. 36" x 42.5". *Courtesy of Beverly Goodrich.*

"Mermaids and Mussels—Circle of Friends." "Each one of these mermaids represents a very special woman in my life: my mother, my grandmother, my sister, my daughters, and my friends." A mussel shell border encircles twelve sea-loving females and a baby. Designed and hooked by Susie Stephenson. Maine. 2005. Diameter 39". *Courtesy of Susie Stephenson.*

Hooked mermaid images not only appear on floors and walls but make charming book covers as well. "Single Mermaid." Adorned with beads and buttons and free flowing yarn tresses. Designed and hooked by Susie Stephenson. Maine. 2005. 14" x 10". *Courtesy of Susie Stephenson.*

"Geneva, the Mermaid" frolics with her deep sea friends. A rolling wave border frames the watery scene. Designed and hooked by Nancy L. Brown. New Hampshire. 2004. 22" x 33". *Courtesy of Nancy L. Brown.*

Detail of "Geneva, the Mermaid" reveals a hooked head of hair enhanced with strands of yarn and a bead-embellished belly button. *Courtesy of Nancy L. Brown.*

Voluptuous mermaids, with bodies hooked from cut strips of panty hose, frolic about while keeping watch over the "Lighthouse Keeper" as he rows home. An angry wife waits ashore, wondering where her sea-going husband has been. Note the artist's initials hooked into smoke rising from the chimney. Designed and hooked by Susie Stephenson. Maine. 2005. 24.5" x 35". *Courtesy of Susie Stephenson.*

"Whirlpool." Churning waters of monochromatic shades of blue. Designed by Pearl McGown. W. Cushing and Company pattern. Hooked by Nola A. Heidbreder. Missouri. 1999. 23.5" x 35". *Courtesy of Nola A. Heidbreder.*

During walks with her husband, Suzan Farrens spotted giant kelp washed in on the Monterey Bay shore. The artist immortalized the ocean vegetation with her hook and colorful strips of woolen fabric. "Gary's Kelp." Designed and hooked by Suzan Farrens. California. 2001. 77" x 20". *Courtesy of Suzan Farrens.*

Cats

In addition to being beloved pets, cats, domestic and wild, are known for having an independent spirit. Rug hookers feel the kinship and love to hook images of their favorite felines.

"This is the story of my beloved cat who lived outside my door for nine years. Whenever I gardened, she was right there with me. She also kept the ground squirrel population in check and chased butterflies. She had the freedom to roam six acres and greeted all who came to the door." A subtle scalloped sky and bright fantasy flowers form a backdrop for Molly as she steps beyond the confines of her rug's frame. "Molly in the Garden." Designed and hooked by Suzanne S. Hamer. Illinois. 2004. 23" x 32". *Courtesy of Suzanne S. Hamer.*

A multicolored quilt-like backdrop sets the stage for a seated and watchful Stripey. The artist hooked this cat's portrait as a gift for her granddaughter's sixteenth birthday. "For Jilian." Designed and hooked by Suzanne S. Hamer. Illinois. 2002. 36" x 26". *Courtesy of Suzanne S. Hamer.*

"Ode to Purple Cat." Only a purple kitty would leave turquoise paw prints. The hooking artist changed the pre-printed pattern's background, then added a border and paw prints. Hooked on the Creek pattern. Hooked by Eleanor de Vecchis. New York. 2004. 27.5" x 19.5" *Courtesy of Eleanor de Vecchis.*

A hooked rug that every cat loving quilter would adore. "Patchwork Cat" poses against a crazy quilt background. DiFranza Designs pattern. Hooked by Fran Oken. Vermont. 1999. 35" x 27.5". *Courtesy of Fran Oken.*

"This was a joint venture with my mother. I sketched 'Blackie and George' from life and my mother designed the background. Then she hooked the entire rug herself." Designed by Jean Conrad Johnson. Hooked by Lettie Conrad. Vermont. 1995. 30" x 41". *Courtesy of Lettie Conrad and Jean Conrad Johnson.*

Oh…the travels this Gulliver must have seen. After he appeared at her doorstep one winter's day, Donna Armour, with the help of a veterinarian, nursed the frightfully ill, newly named Gulliver back to health. In return, she and friend Carol White were rewarded for the next twelve years with feline loyalty, affection, and companionship. In his portrait, the once feral cat wears his purple collar and tags. Adapted from "Tabby Cat." Designed by Joan Moshimer. W. Cushing and Company pattern. Hooked by Donna M. Armour. Rhode Island. 2004. 22" x 20". *Courtesy of Donna M. Armour.*

"Dancer." Grandson Bill's cat is immortalized on a hooked pillow cover. Designed and hooked by Suzanne S. Hamer. Illinois. 2001. 11.5" x 10". *Courtesy of Suzanne S. Hamer.*

"Cozy Cat." Stretched out and stress-free. Designed by Chris Lewis. Dogwood Hooked Art pattern. Hooked by Ariel Baker. Missouri. 1997. Diameter 14.5". *Courtesy of Ariel Baker- Dogwood Hooked Art.*

Kitsa and Pumpkin, once mortal enemies, cuddle up together for an afternoon snooze. "Going Round and Round" was fiber artist Judy Dodds' first attempt at hooking. Designed and hooked by Judy Dodds. Vermont. 2001. Diameter 17". *Courtesy of Judy Dodds.*

Me? What bird? I didn't do a thing. Honoring an incredible appetite, a satiated Max reclines on his tasseled pillow after the big catch. "The Max." Designed and hooked by Carol W. Murphy. New Hampshire. 1995. 30" x 42". *Courtesy of Carol W. Murphy.*

A playful Widget; tangled up in yarn and loving it. Photographs of the artist's cat were used to modify and personalize a pattern from an old *McCall's* magazine. "Mischievous Cat." Designer unknown. Hooked by Jean S. Vogel. Oregon. 2004. 24" x 36". *Courtesy of Jean S. Vogel.*

Contented Zoomie dons a bright red ribbon to match his ball of yarn. "Cat and Ball." Lib Callaway pattern / Hook Nook. Hooked by Barbara Holt Hussey. New Hampshire. 2003. 29" x 40.5". *Courtesy of Barbara Holt Hussey.*

To be surrounded by mice...now that's "The Cat's Meow." Tribute is paid to Hobson, a fine cat and an experienced hunter. Swift paws venture into the mouse border. Primco pattern. Hooked by Susan Higgins. California. 2005. 20" x 30". *Courtesy of Susan Higgins.*

Detail of "The Cat's Meow." *Courtesy of Susan Higgins.*

Shirlee Miller was inspired to hook "Kitty" after viewing an engraving at New York's Metropolitan Museum of Art. The primitive feline rests on a striated field of green. Adapted from a postcard image. Hooked by Shirlee Miller. Massachusetts. 1996. 34" x 42". *Courtesy of Shirlee Miller.*

"Bob's Theo." Found in the blueberry bushes, Theo immediately became attached to Bob. The opinionated cat howls whenever Bob leaves the house and barely tolerates his rug hooking wife. Adapted from "Paisley Cat." Quail Hill Designs pattern. Hooked by Jeni Nunnally. Maine. 2005. 28" x 37". *Courtesy of Jeni Nunnally.*

Geometric patterns set the stage for a demure kitty as he peers out upon his audience. "Olde Cat." Woolley Fox pattern. Hooked by Benita H. Seip. Pennsylvania. 2003. 31" x 23". *Courtesy of Benita H. Seip.*

Contented and well fed. No need to chase this brave mouse. "Lazy Cat." Designed and hooked by Betsy Gerakaris. Connecticut. 2002. 24" x 33". *Courtesy of Betsy Gerakaris.*

"Lena and Friends." "This rug immortalizes my pets: Lena, the cat; Thing 1 and Thing 2, the fish; and my four ferrets, Pippa, Emmett, Tucker, and Lucy. Due to size constraints, bones symbolize our dogs." Designed and hooked by Melissa A. Day. Rhode Island. 2004. 18" x 24". *Courtesy of Melissa A. Day.*

Abandoned in the woods when they were about five months old, "Jay and Paka" lived happily ever after for thirteen years with this kindhearted rug hooker and her family. Designed and hooked by Gail Majauckas. Massachusetts. 2004. 19" x 30". *Courtesy of Gail Majauckas.*

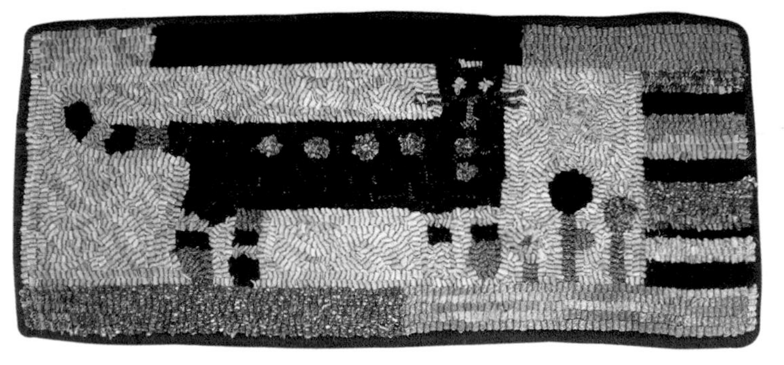

A fun piece to hook. "Itty Bitty Kitty." Vermont Folk Rugs pattern. Hooked by Hildegarde Edling. New York. 2003. 8.5" x 20". *Courtesy of Hildegarde Edling.*

"Field Play." Three feline faces and two frightened mice compose a whimsical banner. In addition to hooking with strips of woolen fabric, the artist used strips of cut up panty hose. The trio's whiskers were hooked with nylon filament. Designed and hooked by Patsy Spitta. California. 2003. 10" x 53". *Courtesy of Patsy Spitta.*

"Hypnotic—Blue #1." Piercing eyes keep watch. Designed and hooked by Karen Balon. New Hampshire. 2004. 12" x 20.5". *Courtesy of Art in the Wool by Karen Balon.*

Intense eyes follow your every move. "Tiger, Tiger." Designed by Jane McGown Flynn. House of Price / Charco pattern. Hooked by Suzanne S. Hamer. Illinois. 1998. 16" x 18.5". *Courtesy of Suzanne S. Hamer.*

Native motifs complement the king of the jungle's portrait. "Boumt Je." Designed and hooked by Judy Fresk. Connecticut. 2000. 33" x 29.5". *Courtesy of Judy Fresk.*

"Crown Prince." With mirror in hand, a pet monkey tries to show a princely leopard his own reflection. The feline royalty sports a velvet coat, regal crown, and carries a walking stick. His companion dons a court jester's hat. Hooking artist Susan Naples, using her hook and strips of woolen fabric, has successfully mastered the difficult task of visually conveying the tactile qualities of the animals' fur and the lushness of the clothing. Hues and Views pattern. Hooked by Susan Naples. California. 2003. 31.5" x 21.5". *Courtesy of Susan Naples.*

Above right and right:
Details of "Crown Prince."
Courtesy of Susan Naples.

Jacob loved watching his grandmother hook "his" carpet. Susan Naples' goal was to create a rug that would grow with her grandson and not be considered too juvenile after a few years. Fantasy flowers and foliage surround a stylized leopard and tiger. The "Tumbling Cats" pre-printed rug pattern is adapted from a design by Dahlov Ipcar. Maker unknown. Hooked by Susan Naples. California. 2002. 27.5" x 36.5". *Courtesy of Susan Naples.*

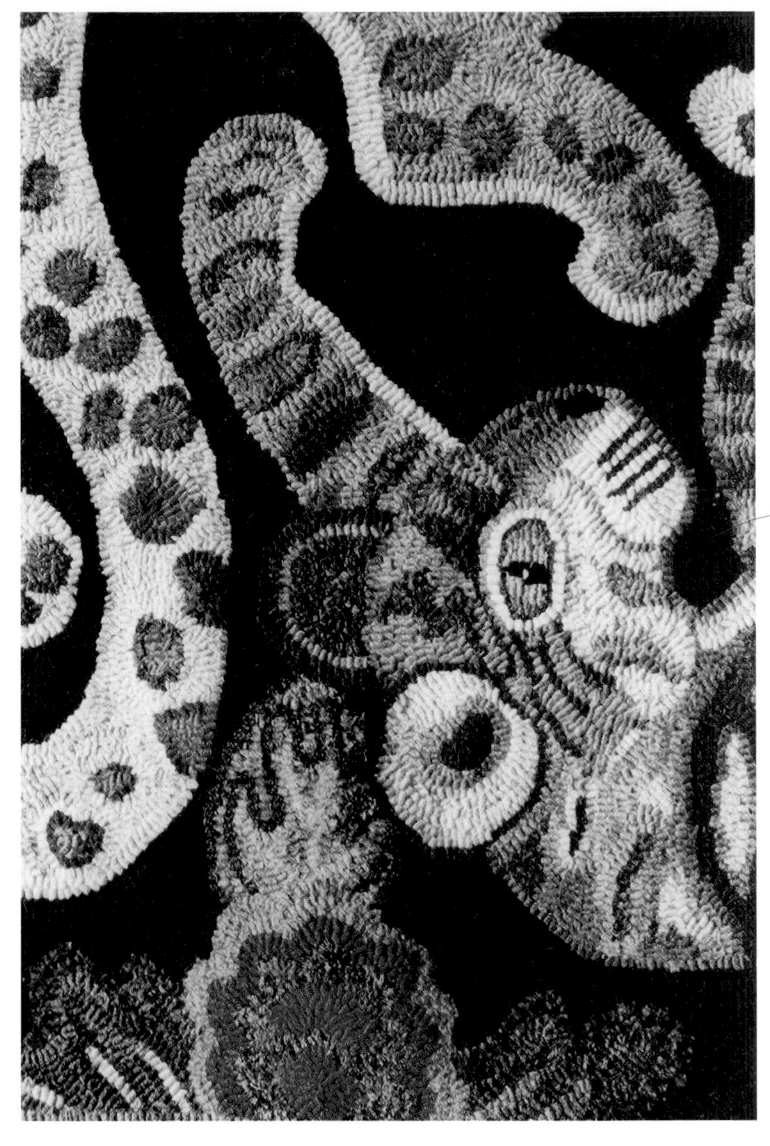

Detail of "Tumbling Cats." *Courtesy of Susan Naples.*

Another interpretation of Dahlov Ipcar's design of exotic cats frolicking in imaginary jungle vegetation. The dark background intensifies vibrant colors. "Tumbling Cats" pattern. Maker unknown. Hooked by Joan Mohrmann. New York. 2003. 28" x 42". *Courtesy of Joan Mohrmann.*

Anna King

Dubbed the "Pottery Capital of the World," the Seagrove area of North Carolina is home to hundreds of men and women who continue a tradition started over two hundred years ago. Using local clays, third and fourth generation potters hand-turn traditional stoneware and wood fired salt glazed works of art. Anna King, her husband Terry, and their daughter Crystal, true to their heritage, produce some of the area's finest and most sought after pottery and art pieces. Away from her potter's wheel, Anna designs, hooks, and sells rugs.

Seagrove, North Carolina, a haven for pottery lovers. Brochure maps lead the way to hundreds of shops including local favorite, King's Pottery.

Potter and rug hooker Anna King stands beside the 12' x 10' rug that she designed and is currently working on. Hand prints separate images of the unique hand-thrown pottery that she, husband Terry, and daughter Crystal create, including their signature face jugs. "King's Pottery Memory Rug." Designed and hooked by Anna King. North Carolina. 2005. 12' x 10'. *Photo by Tim Ayers. Courtesy of Anna King.*

Hooked Fantasy

What better way to escape the trials and tribulations of today's world than with your hook and imagination.

"Rain Forest Dream" was inspired by the artist's travels to faraway lands. Southeast Asian birds, flowers, and reptiles provide cover for a watchful tiger. Designed and hooked by Ann Winterling. New Hampshire. 2004. 35.5" x 43". *Courtesy of Ann Winterling.*

Images of "Green Man," a mythical being dating back to the druids, were found throughout Europe—lurking about on ancient cathedrals, shrines, and castles. In more modern times, his face has appeared on cement garden ornaments. Faith Webster softens a threatening gargoyle with fruit, flowers, and gold-tipped leaves. Note the contoured shape of this unique piece. Designed and hooked by Faith Webster. Maine. 2000. 20" x 14". *Courtesy of Faith Webster.*

Living in harmony in a tropical paradise. "Francis Fantasy." Prairie Craft House pattern. Hooked by Minerva D. Cabanas. Kansas. 2004. 39" x 30". *Courtesy of Minerva D. Cabanas.*

"This rug was inspired by memories of moving back to Connecticut after living in the city for seven years. What stands out in my mind is a big bunch of beautiful zinnias that my mother gave me from her garden on a bright summer morning. Also, the sounds of the birds in the early spring. Their singing can be heard through partially opened windows even before daylight." "Pure Joy." Designed and hooked by Liz Alpert Fay. Connecticut. 2003. 54" x 43". *Courtesy of Liz Alpert Fay.*

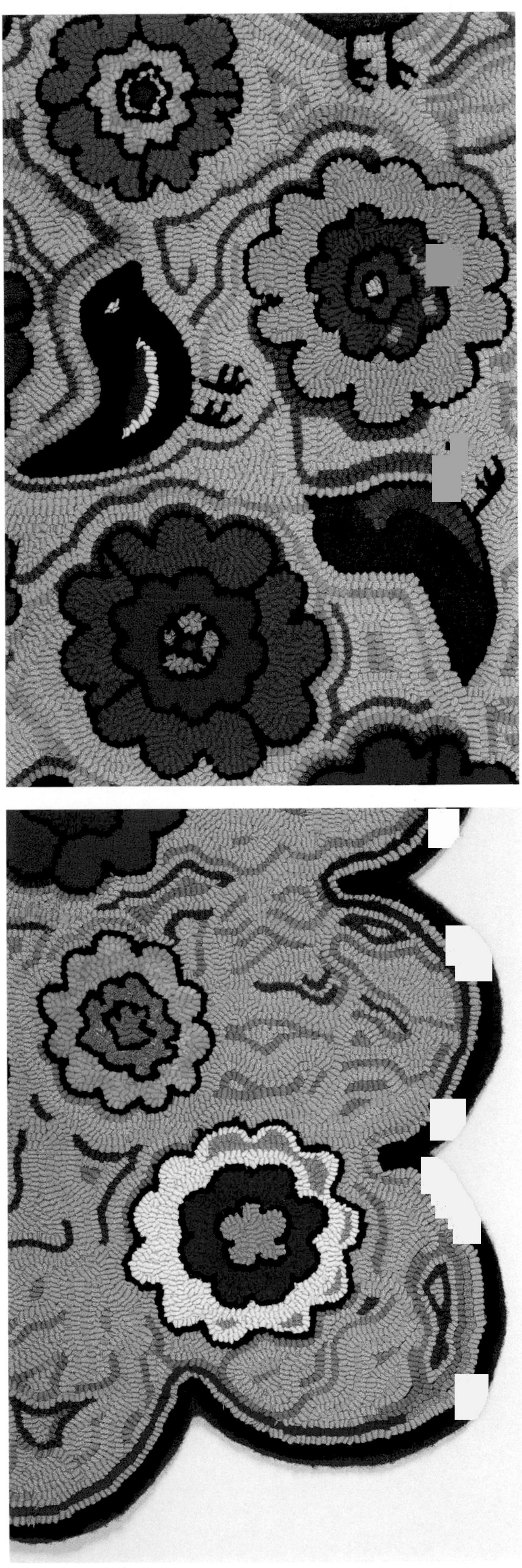

Details of "Pure Joy." *Courtesy of Liz Alpert Fay.*

"A few years ago my sister-in-law, who is an artist, made me a 'sun' bowl out of papier mâche. In the middle of the bowl, she painted the white of the sun and it moved out to the edges in an orange flame. When you flipped the bowl over, it was dark purple/blue with stars all over it. I loved it and wanted to use the concept in a rug. When I created 'Sky Dragon,' the border became a 'sun' border that begins in the upper right hand corner. The sun shines all around into the night sky in the bottom left corner. For interest, I had sunbeams break out of the border into the picture. They almost look like dragon claws. The moon breaks into the sun border. It creates a circle of life." The dragon's three-dimensional scaled body was achieved by raising and sculpting the hooked loops. Designed and hooked by Carolyn Kilner. Ontario, Canada. 1999. 60" x 50". *Courtesy of Carolyn Kilner.*

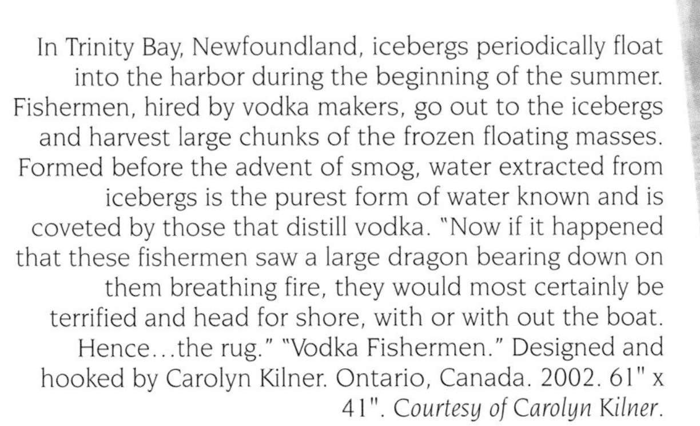

In Trinity Bay, Newfoundland, icebergs periodically float into the harbor during the beginning of the summer. Fishermen, hired by vodka makers, go out to the icebergs and harvest large chunks of the frozen floating masses. Formed before the advent of smog, water extracted from icebergs is the purest form of water known and is coveted by those that distill vodka. "Now if it happened that these fishermen saw a large dragon bearing down on them breathing fire, they would most certainly be terrified and head for shore, with or with out the boat. Hence…the rug." "Vodka Fishermen." Designed and hooked by Carolyn Kilner. Ontario, Canada. 2002. 61" x 41". *Courtesy of Carolyn Kilner.*

Detail of "Vodka Fishermen." *Courtesy of Carolyn Kilner.*

Leaves

Foliage takes center stage, uprooting the ever popular hooked flower.

In the shape of that it portrays. "Oak Leaf" was hooked using one piece of woolen fabric dyed with six different colors. Once cut into strips, Sharon Saknit was able to hook from the base of the leaf to the tip with color changes occurring naturally. Designed and hooked by Sharon Saknit. California. 2004. 8" x 14.5". *Courtesy of Sharon Saknit.*

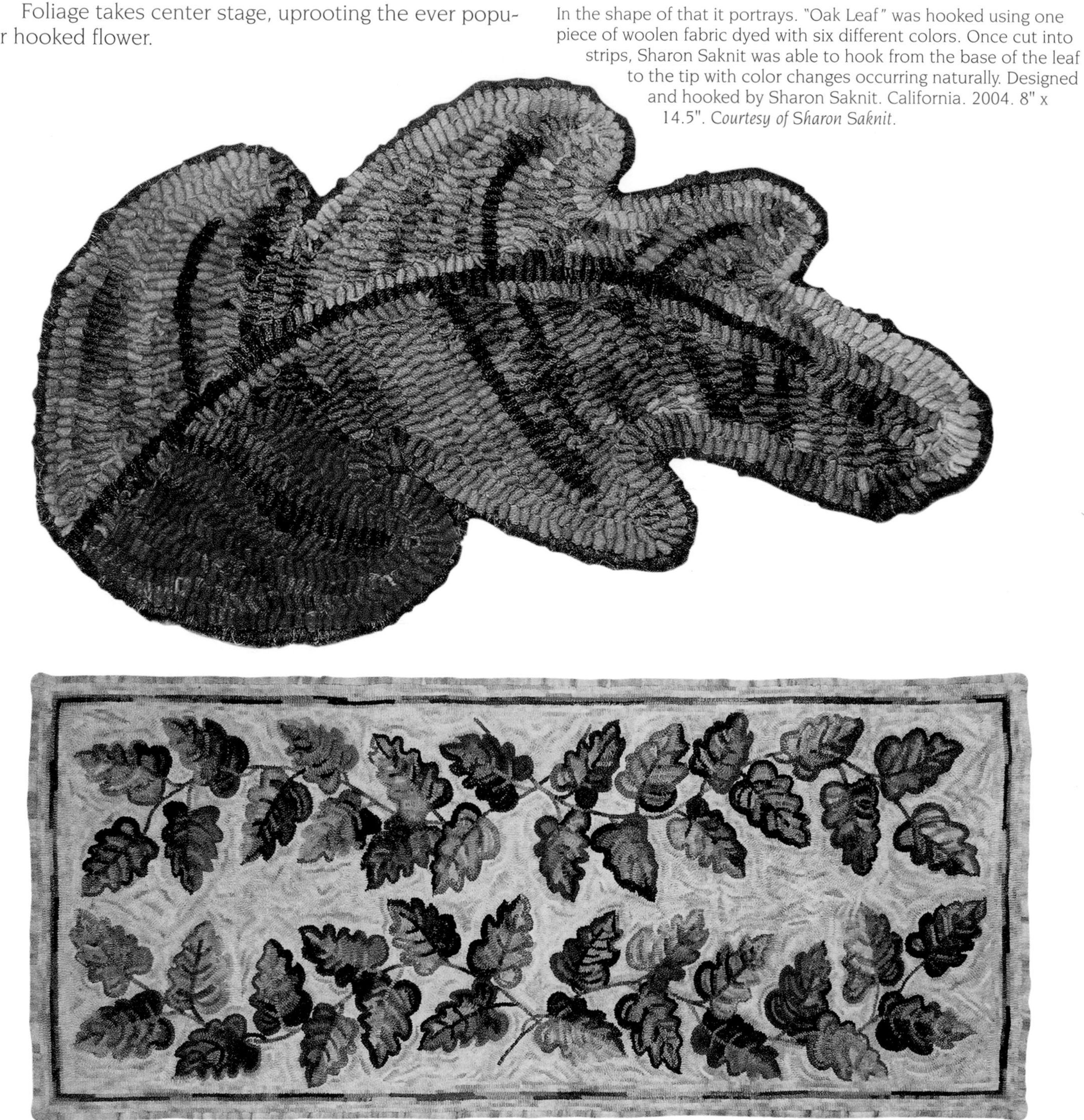

"I took the outline of six leaves from an antique rug pattern and arranged them onto four intersecting vines. "Falling Leaves." Adapted from an antique rug pattern. Designed and hooked by Sharon Saknit. California. 2004. 27.5" x 62.5". *Courtesy of Sharon Saknit.*

A flame stitch background highlights a single leaf, hooked from sixteen different hand-dyed shades of woolen fabric. "Powder Room Scroll." Adapted from a wallpaper border. Hooked by Sharon Saknit. California. 2000. 18" x 24". *Courtesy of Sharon Saknit*.

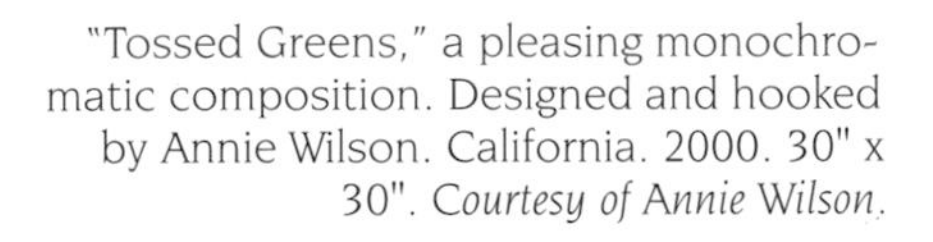

"Tossed Greens," a pleasing monochromatic composition. Designed and hooked by Annie Wilson. California. 2000. 30" x 30". *Courtesy of Annie Wilson*.

"I wanted a rug that looked like a pile of autumn leaves." The woolen fabric used by hooking artist Joyce Krueger was dip-dyed, onion skin-dyed, casserole-dyed, swatch-dyed, and as is. "Autumn Leaf Puzzle." Designed and hooked by Joyce Krueger. Wisconsin. 2004. 39.5" x 28". *Courtesy of Joyce Krueger.*

"'Ferns' is reminiscent of the woodland fern beds that I knew from my childhood summers in Pennsylvania. I can so vividly recall walking through the woods and experiencing the surprise of coming upon a bed of ferns. The sudden change from deep dense woods to the openness and intense green of the fern bed invariably made me pause. I would stop to feel the warmth and glow of the sun and take in every aspect of the moment. 'Ferns' is my attempt to capture that moment... my memories of the broken sunlight falling upon an intricate layering of ferns. The dark and mysterious, combined with hot spots of color and warmth." Designed and hooked by Susan Higgins. California 1996. 22" x 30". *Courtesy of Susan Higgins.*

Detail of "Ferns." Note the tiny salamander. *Courtesy of Susan Higgins.*

A collage of colorful leaves arranged in a reverse image pattern. "Leaves Too." Designed by Annie Wilson. Hooked by Betty Magan. California. 2005. 64" x 42". *Courtesy of Betty Magan.*

A work in progress. Annie Wilson hooks her own interpretation of the aforementioned "Leaves Too" pattern. Designed and hooked by Annie Wilson. California. 2005. 64" x 42". *Courtesy of Annie Wilson.*

Hooked in a limited color scheme, "Autumn" leaves and acorns head in all directions on this rug. Designed and hooked by Eleanor de Vecchis. New York. 2004. 29.5" x 39". *Courtesy of Eleanor de Vecchis.*

Joined branches of leaves form an oval wreath. Using the neutral background colors, Anna Boyer hooked a barely visible floral motif in the center of her rug. Adapted from an old rug pattern featured in a 1932 *Women's Day* magazine. Hooked by Anna Boyer. California. 2002. 32" x 53". *Courtesy of Anna Boyer.*

Detail from the underside of the aforementioned rug shows the floral motif that Anna Boyer hooked into the background. *Courtesy of Anna Boyer.*

"I found this pre-colored pattern in an antique shop in New Hampshire. The leaves had various fall colors so I started collecting wool that would look like the colors on the pattern. I chose a dark background and dyed the wool myself. This was my first rug and first dyeing project. I finished my rug the first fall I moved to Vermont." "Fall in Vermont." Dritz pattern. Hooked by Elizabeth Morgan. Vermont. 1999. 35" x 51". *Courtesy of Elizabeth Morgan.*

Inspired by plastic leaf decals stuck on school windows, the "Marriage of Earth and Sky" captures an array of fallen leaves and suspends them in mid air. Designed and hooked by Kathy T. Stephens. Montana. 2005. 23" x 34". *Courtesy of Kathy T. Stephens.*

A border knit with chenille, homespun, and wool yarns frames a "Funky Autumn" collage. Designed and hooked by Nola A. Heidbreder. Missouri. 2004. 14" x 16.5". *Courtesy of Nola A. Heidbreder.*

The gold and orange colors of autumn leaves command attention. "Autumn Rhythm." Designed by Pearl McGown. W. Cushing and Company pattern. Hooked by Andrea Scott Trout. Rhode Island. 2002. 58" x 32". *Courtesy of Andrea Scott Trout.*

Fall leaves artistically scattered on a rich dark background. "Porcelain." Designed by Pearl McGown. W. Cushing and Company pattern. Hooked by Janet Bosshard. New Jersey. 2004. 28" x 46". *Courtesy of Janet Bosshart.*

Amid tree tops, the face of a mysterious man appears. "Spring—Summer—Fall." Designed and hooked by Annie Wilson. California. 2003. 19" x 25". *Courtesy of Annie Wilson.*

Commemorative Hookings

Rugs hookers often create works that commemorate that which is near and dear or life changing.

"This is my 9/11 mourning piece." "Broken." Designed and hooked by Anne-Marie Littenberg. Vermont. 2002. Each panel 24" x 18". *Courtesy of Anne-Marie Littenberg.*

"After the tragedy of 9/11, my artwork, both painting and hooking, turned to a red, white and blue theme. I painted six paintings and hooked this one rug in memory of the Twin Towers and love of my country." While attending a hooking workshop at the Shelburne Museum in Vermont, Gloria Reynolds was taken by the ever present American flags and the many gnarled trees that graced the property. She incorporated these images, along with a rainbow, heart, stars, and a bird of peace, in her haunting "Memories of Shelburne Museum." Designed and hooked by Gloria Reynolds. Vermont. 2003. 26" x 24". *Courtesy of Gloria Reynolds.*

"How I coped with 9-11-01." "My husband was scheduled for surgery on 9-12-01. The surgery was postponed and then rescheduled. I drew this design and hooked it at the hospital while he recuperated. It helped me cope with my husband's illness and the horrific images on TV at the time." Designed and hooked by Susan Andreson. California. 2001. 12" x 16". *Courtesy of Susan Andreson.*

"This is my patriotic rug. I decided I needed to make one after 9/11." Adapted from the folk art of Margaret Shaw. Kris Miller / Spruce Ridge Studios pattern. Hooked by Fran Romig. Pennsylvania. 2003. 26" x 36". *Courtesy of Fran Romig.*

"Hooked in memory of the victims of 9-11-01. The two large stars represent the Twin Towers of the World Trade Center. The smaller ones are for the Pentagon and the plane that crashed in Pennsylvania." "My Star Spangled Rug." Designed and hooked by Gail Majauckas. Massachusetts. 2002. 24" x 36". *Courtesy of Gail Majauckas.*

"I did this when laid up with a broken ankle and while on the sofa watching the endless news coverage of 9/11." Designed and hooked by Debbie Torre. Rhode Island. 2001. 19" x 44". *Courtesy of Debbie Torre.*

"I hooked this piece while my husband was half a world away." The crane symbolizes love and commitment, the sun and the moon represent the miles that separate. Inspired by a Korean china pattern. "My Love is in Korea." Designed and hooked by Michelle M. Weaver. Michigan. 2004. 28" x 33". *Courtesy of Michelle M. Weaver.*

"My partner Annette and her sister Marie both dealt with cancer the same year. Upon completion of their treatments, Marie and her husband Nels and Annette and I toured Alaska. It was Marie's trip of a lifetime—a dream come true. Jane Olson (rug hooking artist, designer, and teacher) drew up the pattern based on my photo and desires. It was perfect. I gave the framed piece to Marie for Christmas the following year. She suffered a recurrence of cancer in 2003 and sadly passed away. 'Orca-Stra' now resides in our home, a loving memory of a great trip and a wonderful woman." Designed by Jane Olson. Hooked by Susan Naples. California. 1999. 32" x 26". *Courtesy of Susan Naples.*

Detail of "Orca-Stra." *Courtesy of Susan Naples.*

Detail of "Orca-Stra." The reflected image of the whale incorporates a Native Northwestern design. *Courtesy of Susan Naples.*

"For me, there are many philosophical aspects to the design of this piece. The title 'Going Home' was conceived because I looked at this view as a passageway. The land beneath this stormy sky is a lovely valley near Gillett Grove, Iowa. My husband and I pass through it most every time we go back home to visit. I took the artistic liberty of putting in a couple of southern Iowa terraces in the lower left hand corner, as we were long time Council Bluffs residents and I consider that place also home. The tree area on the right is a view of the old Garfield Cemetery where my husband's parents are laid to rest, another homecoming. The land area signifies what can be physically be touched. The sky is another matter. The stormy upper clouds and rain are sadness, loss, and disagreements, while the beautiful sunlit clouds are symbolic of happy times, blessings, and togetherness. The road between them is love, and this is what keeps leading us home." Inspired by the works of landscape painter, Marvin Cone, "Going Home" took about six hundred hours to complete. Designed and hooked by Liala Ralph. Iowa. 2001. 25" x 35". *Courtesy of Liala Ralph.*

Detail of "Going Home."
Courtesy of Liala Ralph.

"The border of this rug is a typical 'Azeri' border. I changed the interior to fit 'my story.' The hills are reminiscent of the Highland Hills that I photographed during our trip to Scotland. Being my totem, the hawk is always with me. I put in the mother with her three babies and hooked the babies from bird feathers. Also pictured is the log home we built twenty-eight years ago from the trees on the property. Ravens were placed around the rug symbolizing the family of ravens that built a nest in our tree three years ago. A few months later, our granddaughter was born and she is named Brenna. Brenna means raven in Gaelic. In the pond float my mother, brother, sister, and me. Rowan, my cat, stands guard. The cardinal symbolizes the spirit of a very close friend's mother who passed on a few years ago." Adapted from "Azeri." Designed by Jane McGown Flynn. House of Price / Charco pattern. Hooked by Jan Seavey. New Hampshire. 2005. 42" x 27". *Courtesy of Jan Seavey.*

"Desert Memories." "This hooking came about after my husband Chuck and I took a trip to Death Valley in our fifth wheel trailer and came back with books on desert mammals and wild flowers. On the way back to our home, on the Nipomo Mesa in California, I was already determined to plant a cactus garden and to hook a desert memory rug." Designed by Elizabeth Black. Hooked by Sandra Harris. California. 2004. 22" x 25". *Courtesy of Sandra Harris.*

Robert Cheatley is a devoted friend who gave of himself when Susan Andreson's husband underwent lung surgery. "He sat with me at the hospital, helped John and me with doctors, told us what to expect, came every day, and provided us with hope, information, and faith. I designed this rug to show our guardian angel that he is a star in our firmament. He is a survivor of six-way heart bypass and is active in 'Mended Hearts'—hence the heart that is stitched. He drives a 1937 Ford, played pro-football, and loves basketball." "Cheat's Rug—From Susan's Heart." Designed and hooked by Susan Andreson. California. 2001. 24" x 30". *Courtesy of Susan Andreson.*

"My Plans for You." "This piece expressed my thoughts for the new millennium. I chose the particular scripture because it is so strongly positive for the future." Designed and hooked by Chris Lewis. Missouri. 2000. 15" x 21". *Courtesy of Chris Lewis - Dogwood Hooked Art.*

Depicted are six generations of Marilyn Schmidt's family—"from my great-grandfather Patrick Darby in the Andersonville prison during the Civil War to my grandchildren." A full teaching schedule left Marilyn unable to devote as much time to her own hooking as desired; hence this impressive commemorative work took six years to complete. "Schmidt–Moore Family Album Rug." Designed by Emma Lou Lais and Marilyn Schmidt. Hooked by Marilyn Schmidt. Kansas. 1997. 9' x 6'. *Courtesy of Marilyn Schmidt.*

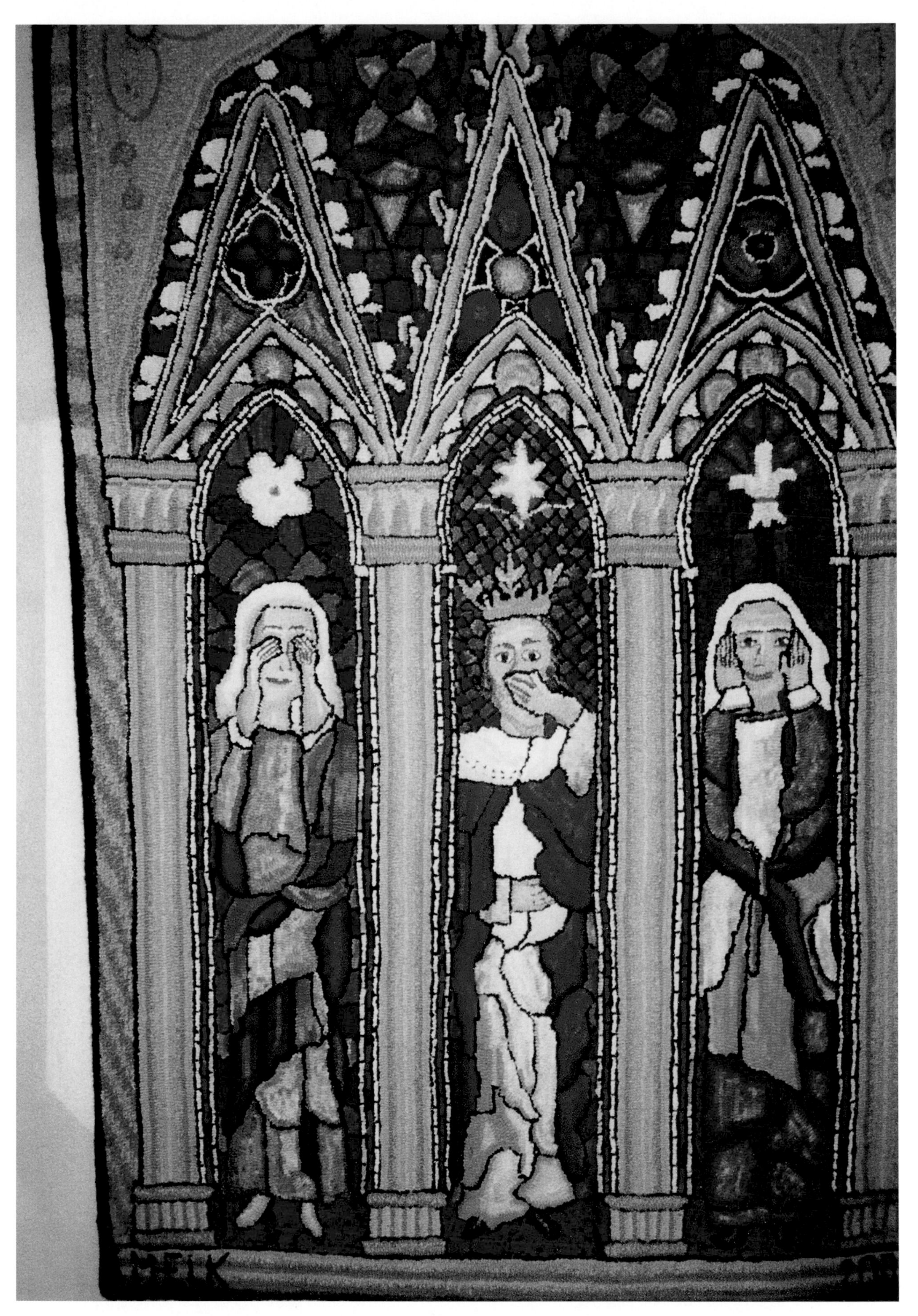

"The Gossips." See no evil. Speak no evil. Hear no evil. "My daughter is a medieval church historian and this was made for her." Designed and hooked by Beth Kempf. Connecticut. 2003. 70" x 44". *Courtesy of Beth Kempf.*

"I have hooked a rug for each of my grandchildren, who are one year apart in age. When the oldest, Jacob, saw this pattern he said, 'Angie and Hannah are in the rug…where is me?' So Diane Stoffel (rug hooking artist and teacher) drew him in the tree." "Best Friends." Pris Buttler Rug Designs pattern. Hooked by Susan Naples. California. 2003. 26.5" x 36.5". *Courtesy of Susan Naples.*

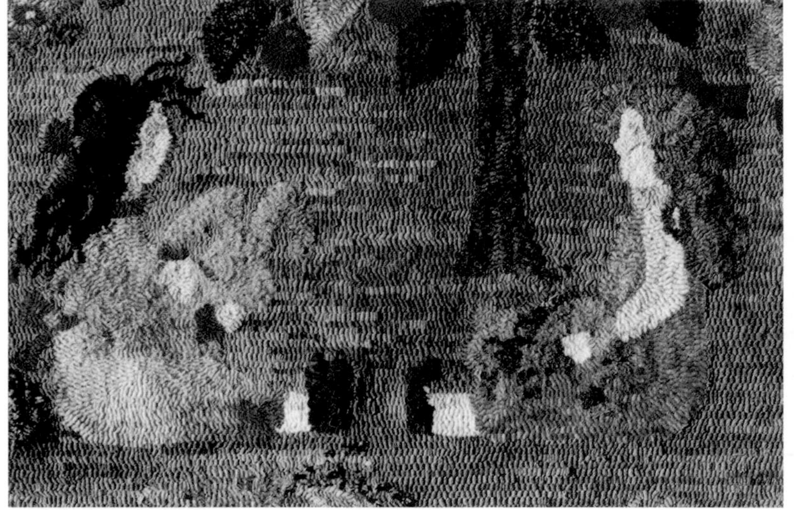

Detail of "Best Friends." *Courtesy of Susan Naples.*

Detail of "Best Friends," showing Jacob sitting in the tree. *Courtesy of Susan Naples.*

"The 'Pals' pattern was chosen because of the pair of elephants. These represent my friend and myself, who, though we have lived miles apart and have lived different lives, 'never forget.' The design and colors seem to capture the playfulness and good times we've shared." Beverly Conway Designs pattern. Hooked by Nancy E. Baker. Vermont. 2004. 14" x 21". *Courtesy of Nancy E. Baker.*

"This 'School House Rug' was hooked for my husband, Stephen, who is the principal of the Aquidneck Christian Academy in Portsmouth, Rhode Island. The rug was presented as a gift upon his appointment as principal of the school. This rug has been enjoyed (and walked on) by many children in our home and, for a short time, at the school!" Designed by Joan Moshimer. W. Cushing and Company pattern. Hooked by Susan Bailey. Rhode Island.1999. 33" x 43". *Courtesy of Susan Bailey.*

"Ron Hard at Work." "This rug was hooked to commemorate the auction company my husband owns and operates as well as the year (2004) he spent as president of the Maine Auctioneers Association." Designed and hooked by Lisanne Miller, Maine. 2004. 41" x 31". *Courtesy of Lisanne Miller*

Cranberry Rug Hookers Exhibit

The Cranberry Rug Hookers chapter of ATHA (Association of Traditional Hooking Artists), formed in 1990, brings together hooking artists from the South Shore, Cape Cod, and the Island regions of Massachusetts. In October 2004, the group sponsored a much anticipated and well-attended exhibit of their members' work.

The Massachusetts Cranberry Chapter of the ATHA (Association of Traditional Hooking Artists) announce their much anticipated 2004 exhibit. *Courtesy of the Cranberry Hookers Guild.*

On display were hooked rugs of every shape, size, and subject. *Courtesy of the Cranberry Rug Hookers Guild.*

"Chimera." Dream-like animals float in a fantasy floral garden. Bold borders frame the center motif. New Earth Designs pattern. Hooked by Dulany Osler. Massachusetts. 1996. 54" x 40". *Courtesy of Dulany Osler.*

"This is my first in a series of rugs I intend to adapt from seventy-eight historic United States events documented over a thirty year period by American painter / historian J. L. G. Ferris (1863-1930). Mr. Ferris spent thirty years of his life researching and creating these paintings and chose not to sell them, but rather to keep them together as one body of work."

"Writing the Declaration of Independence, 1776." Adapted from a 1921 painting by J. L. G. Ferris with permission from his heirs. Hooked by Patricia R. White. Massachusetts. 2004. 26" x 19". *Courtesy of Patricia R. White and the heirs of J. L. G. Ferris.*

Inspiration comes from many sources, including this mythical creature spotted on a decorative license plate. "Red Dragon." Designed and hooked by Doreen Holmquist. Massachusetts. 2004. 23.5" x 33.5". *Courtesy of Doreen Holmquist.*

Seated at her frame, Lesa Bregy demonstrates the art of rug hooking. *Courtesy of Lesa Bregy.*

Not all hooked work is made to warm drafty floors or decorate walls. A hooked pumpkin and Indian corn recall a bountiful harvest. Designed and hooked by Lesa Bregy. Maine. Life-size. 2003. *Courtesy of Lisa Bregy.*

"Victorian House." A hooked painted lady. Designed by Ingrid Hieronimus. Hooked by Doris Beatty. Massachusetts. 2003. 21" x 23". *Courtesy of Doris Beatty.*

"Lesa and Alice." Self portrait of a fiery redhead, flowers, and feline friend. Designed and hooked by Lesa Bregy. Maine. 2004. 31" x 16". *Courtesy of Lesa Bregy.*

This quaint imaginary village welcomes all rug hookers. "Houses." Yankee Peddler pattern. Hooked by Doris Beatty. Massachusetts. 2002. 38" x 24". *Courtesy of Doris Beatty.*

"Oriental." A glorious sunset in an exotic land. Adapted from "Oriental Bench Cover." House of Price / Charco pattern. Hooked by Dawn Dykeman. Massachusetts. 2002. 12" x 35". *Courtesy of Dawn Dykeman.*

A picturesque sunset and "A Stop at the Inn" end a perfect winter's day. Adapted from a Currier and Ives print. Designed by Pearl McGown. W. Cushing and Company pattern. Hooked by Jean Snow. Massachusetts. 2002. 27" x 42". *Courtesy of Jean Snow.*

"The Kerosene House." An impressionistic look at an historic Cape Cod structure. Designed and hooked by Dawn Dykeman. Massachusetts. 2002. 12" x 17". *Courtesy of Dawn Dykeman.*

Inspired by Persian-style carpets, a central tree, laden with stylized blossoms, attracts fanciful birds. Note the unique way Norma McElhenny hooked her initials into the base of the tree. "Birds of Sarouk." Designed by Jane McGown Flynn. House of Price/ Charco pattern. Hooked by Norma McElhenny. Massachusetts. 2003. 60" x 42". *Courtesy of Norma McElhenny.*

"I like quilting designs and wanted to work with the traditional log cabin design. I had been driving around New England and wanted to use some of the wonderful fall colors, so I decided to interpret the log cabin into a stylized landscape." "Log Cabin Clearing." Designed and hooked by Peg Irish. Massachusetts. 2004. 21" x 24". *Courtesy of Peg Irish.*

"My Cape Cod House." An imagined ideal home. Designed and hooked by Marian Gray. Massachusetts. 2004. 17" x 17". *Courtesy of Marian Gray.*

Friends, fireworks and "Sail Watching." Who could ask for more? Patsy Becker pattern. Hooked by Carol N. Brown. Massachusetts. 2003. 19" x 27.5". *Courtesy of Carol N. Brown.*

Cleaning up after a successful exhibit. A good time was had by all. *Courtesy of the Cranberry Hookers Guild.*

Birds of a Feather Hook Together

Images of birds, plain or fancy, real or whimsical, are favored by many rug hooking artists.

Bold and bright and graphically pleasing! The body of this proud peacock was hooked from a cut up "as is" Pendleton woolen shirt, his tail from chenille yarn. "Peacock." Port Primitive pattern. Hooked by Nola A. Heidbreder. Missouri. 2004. 24" x 31.5". *Courtesy of Nola A. Heidbreder.*

A lone "Loon" quietly paddles along. Designed by Joan Moshimer. W. Cushing and Company pattern. Hooked by Tricia Tague Miller. New Hampshire. 2004. 20" x 24.5". *Courtesy of Tricia Tague Miller.*

Showing off iridescent plumage. "I think the peacock is one of the most beautiful birds alive." "Tiffany Peacock." House of Price / Charco pattern. Hooked By Patricia J. Chambers. Missouri. 1997. 43.5" x 18". *Courtesy of Patricia J. Chambers.*

Inspired by the many birds near her house, artist Suzan Farrens hooked "Crane" from an impressionistic point of view. Note the smooth transition of colors from reed to sky. Designed and hooked by Suzan Farrens. California. 2001. 42" x 17". *Courtesy of Suzan Farrens.*

Strips of suede and woolen fabric and lengths of yarn were used to hook "Le Quack," a pre-Columbian Aztec design. Designed and hooked by Jocelyn Guindon. Quebec, Canada. 2000. 13.5" x 16". *Courtesy of Jocelyn Guindon.*

"This piece was developed around birds that Laurel [the artist's daughter] worked with, researched, and studied on her way to a degree. The eagle was chosen as the primary bird shape as it is our national symbol and was to portray a protective role. The Kirtland's warbler is at the end of the tail to depict its fragile existence and low population numbers. Being on the tail reminds us how easy it is to loose a species and how important maintaining habitat is to wildlife. The hummingbird is at the neck and near the 'eagle eye' and terrible beak to show the importance of diversity and how all creatures can co-exist. Only part of the chickadee shows because he was an interloper in a netting project designed to save the warbler. We must remember how important it is for us to be good stewards of bird habitat and conservation." "Laurel's Ornithology Journey." Designed and hooked by Diane Moore. Vermont. 1998. 32" x 28". *Courtesy of Diane Moore.*

As winter approaches, turkeys search for food. Adapted from a photograph. "Turkey Scenic." Jacqueline Designs pattern. Hooked by Karen Detrick. Ohio. 2003. 18" x 24". *Courtesy of Karen Detrick.*

A glowing full moon lights up a "Midnight Rendezvous." The silhouetted pair make a dramatic statement. Note the placement of artist's initials and date in the tree trunk. Adapted with permission from a greeting card print by Yoshiko Yamamoto. Hooked by Jeni Nunnally. Maine. 2004. 29" x 29". *Courtesy of Jeni Nunnally.*

Red berries add touches of color throughout. "Crow." New Earth Designs pattern. Hooked by Patricia Laska. Maine. 2004. 16" x 20". *Courtesy of Patricia Laska.*

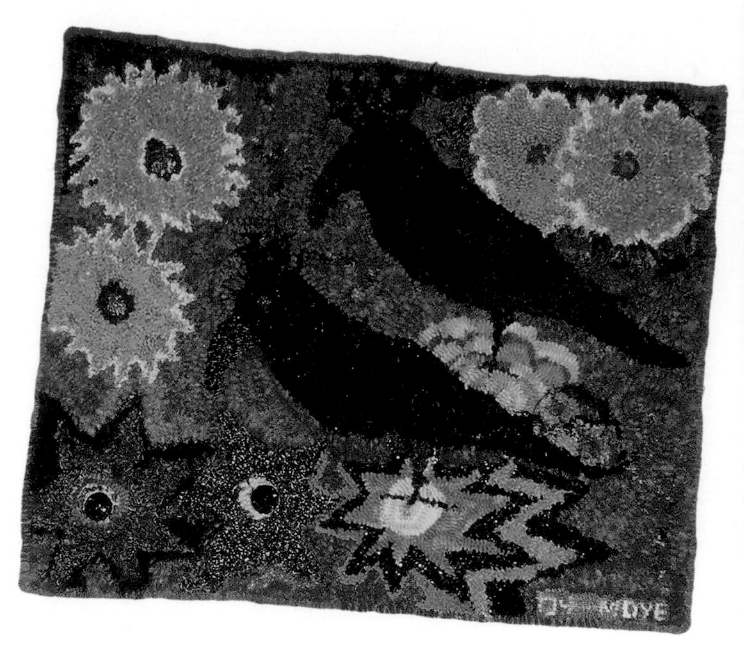

A rug hooker not afraid to try something new. "Our sunny yard is full of crows and I'm really into 'prom' fabrics." Glitz and glamour adorn fashion conscious feathered friends. "All Dressed Up and No Place to Crow." Designed and hooked by Molly W. Dye. Vermont. 2004. 19" x 22". *Courtesy of Molly W. Dye.*

Non-traditional hooking materials such as specialty yarns and shimmering fabrics "are so exciting to work with, it is like sampling a gourmet buffet." "Hail to the Crow." Designed and hooked by Molly W. Dye. Vermont. 2004. 26" x 16". *Courtesy of Molly W. Dye.*

Five forlorn crows line up between stalks of Indian corn and sunflower heads. Polychrome kernels and partial flower heads decorate the rug's outer border. "Crows in the Corn." Adapted from a Harry M. Fraser Company pattern. Hooked by Chris Gooding. Connecticut. 1998. 36" x 48". *Courtesy of Chris Gooding.*

A tiny study of a "Gold Finch Pair." Adapted from a compilation of reference material. Designed and hooked by Marion Wise. California. 2003. 10" x 10". *Courtesy of Marion Wise.*

"Outside the garden room of our 1881 home are large evergreen trees. We have a bird feeder that attracts a large variety of birds, including the chickadee which is one of my favorites. When I saw Pris Buttler's design I decided to bring the outside indoors by hooking this piece. I had a lot of fun doing it and now have the chickadees among my house plants as well as seeing them flutter around outside in the evergreens." "Chickadees." Pris Buttler Rug Designs pattern. Hooked by Benita H. Seip. Pennsylvania. 2004. 15" x 34". *Courtesy of Benita H. Seip.*

Waldoboro-style hooking (raised and sculptured) was used to replicate a circa 1880s rug spotted at a Pennsylvania antique show by rug hooking artist Jacqueline Hansen. The golden color of the scrolls was achieved by dyeing woolen fabric with onion skins. "Waldoboro Bird Floral." Jacqueline Designs pattern. Designed and hooked by Jacqueline Hansen. Maine. 2002. 24" x 36". *Courtesy of Jacqueline Hansen.*

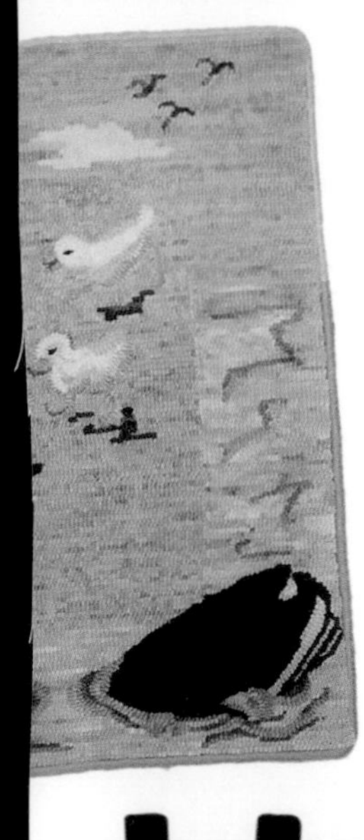

"Ducklings" on land and in the water. Liziana Creations pattern. Hooked by Charlotte Hefford. Maine. 1997. 23.5" x 40". *Courtesy of Charlotte Hefford.*

"Something to Crow About." Rooster feathers and one brave chick venture into the blue block border. Pris Buttler Rug Designs pattern. Hooked by Cathe Evans. Missouri. 2002. 28" x 28". *Courtesy of Cathe Evans.*

Clear skies and delectable goodies…what more could this fine feathered pair ask for? Hooking artist Karen Tate joined forces with multi-talented designer Kaffe Fassett to create her "Westport's Roosters." "Kaffe is delighted that you have found his book *Glorious Inspiration* as a source for your personal inspiration, which is solely what the book was meant for." Designed by Karen Tate and Kaffe Fassett. Hooked by Karen Tate. Massachusetts. 2003. 34" x 48". *Courtesy of Karen Tate.*

Chicken wire keeps fowl in and gives us a glimpse of the world from a feathered point of view. "Chicken Farm Road." Designed and hooked by Beth Kempf. Connecticut. 2002. 33" x 28". *Courtesy of Beth Kempf.*

Always busy from sun up to sun down. "Greetings." Dogwood Hooked Art pattern. Designed and hooked by Chris Lewis. Missouri. 1999. 19" x 34". *Courtesy of Chris Lewis–Dogwood Hooked Art.*

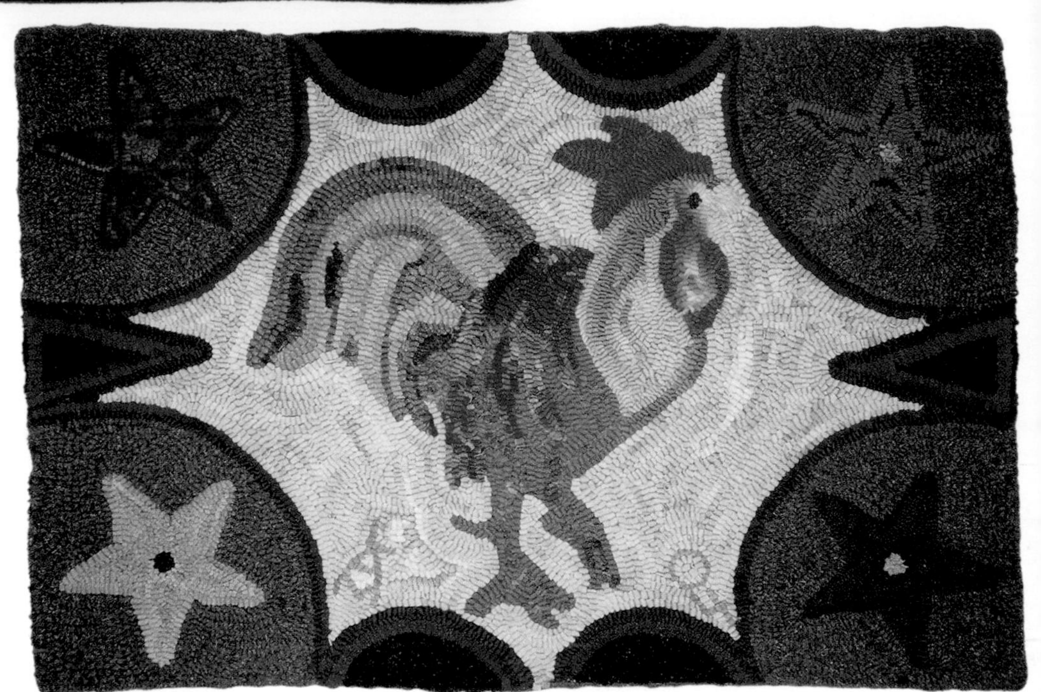

A strutting rooster takes center stage as "Star of the Barn." Designed and hooked by Lisanne Miller. Maine. 2004. 21.5" x 32". *Courtesy of Lisanne Miller.*

Tweeds, plaids, and solid color woolen fabrics were used to hook an abstract background for a "Crazy Quilt Strutter." Designed and hooked by Thelma P. Kirkoff. Pennsylvania. 2004. 26" x 32". *Courtesy of Thelma P. Kirkoff.*

"This plate was a gift from my husband after our first spat. I spent forty-eight years of marriage with many spats and lots of nice apologies." Adapted from a dinner plate design. Hooked by Laura Phinney. Maine. 2004. Diameter 28". *Courtesy of Laura Phinney.*

A series of borders, reminiscent of a Victorian Valentine's Day card, complement "Bird and Berries." Designed by Bea Brock. Hooked by Ann Grover. Texas. 2004. 20" x 24". *Courtesy of Ann Grover.*

"Just Settin' Chicken" was hooked with strips of woolen fabric and specialty yarns. Century old barn boards frame the fancy feathered fowl. Primco pattern. Hooked by Karen Guffey. Iowa. 2002. 20" x 20". *Courtesy of Karen Guffey.*

Six panels, in each a different background and bird, with one "Going Against the Crowd." Adapted from a quilt pattern. Hooked by Polly Reinhart. Pennsylvania. 2001. 33" x 27". *Courtesy of Polly Reinhart.*

Raised, sculptured and hooked in the Waldoboro-style. A three dimensional "Parrot" perches on a budded branch. The overall placement of colors makes for an aesthetically pleasing rug. Adapted from a nineteenth century design. Jacqueline Designs pattern. Hooked by Jeni Nunnally. Maine. 2003. 19" x 28". *Courtesy of Jeni Nunnally.*

Triangles, rectangles, and a zigzag border contain an opposing pair of primitive roosters. "B & B Roosters." Woolley Fox pattern. Hooked by Polly Reinhart. Pennsylvania. 2003. 29" x 45". *Courtesy of Polly Reinhart.*

A wood-like background and solid L brackets enclose an eye-catching swan. Adapted from a carved wooden swan. Hooked by Polly Reinhart. Pennsylvania. 2001. 20" x 26". *Courtesy of Polly Reinhart.*

Polly's Reinhart's rug "Wise" was started in a hooking class at Vermont's Shelburne Museum. The rug's design incorporates items found in and around the museum's buildings, including an owl image modeled after a chalkware figure, a tree motif borrowed from a fire screen, and fiddleheads growing on the property. Designed and hooked by Polly Reinhart. Pennsylvania. 2002. 20" x 26". *Courtesy of Polly Reinhart.*

Persian-, Oriental-, and Woven-style Hooked Rugs

Imitation is the most sincere form of flattery. Rug hookers admire knotted and woven carpets and, since the early days of rug hooking, have created their own versions of the decorative floor coverings.

Stylized flowers and architectural elements radiate out from a central star medallion. Contrasting colors and complementary shades make "Zereh" an exceptional example of a hooked Persian-style rug. Note the addition of knotted fringe. Designed by Jane McGown Flynn. House of Price / Charco pattern. Hooked by Diane Neuse. Vermont. 2001. 56" x 36". *Courtesy of Diane Neuse.*

"Talish." Simple and elegant motifs combine. To mimic the look of a woven Oriental rug, the center field was hooked in a horizontal direction using closely related shades. New Earth Designs pattern. Hooked by Joan Mohrmann. New York. 2000. 108" x 41". *Courtesy of Joan Mohrmann.*

Intricate floral designs and decorative details compose "Sehna." Note the addition of knotted fringe. Designed by Pearl McGown. W. Cushing and Company pattern. Hooked by Doris M. Hennessy. Maine. 2001. 46" x 30". *Courtesy of Doris M. Hennessy.*

Ornamental diamonds, large and small, join an array of geometric designs. "Desert Wander" is reminiscent of the tribal rugs woven by traveling nomads. Designed by Jane McGown Flynn. House of Price / Charco pattern. Hooked by Joyce Krueger. Wisconsin. 1996. 86" x 43". *Courtesy of Joyce Krueger.*

Left:
"Caucasian Camels." The original rug came from the village of Lamberan in Azerbaijan and is now in the Mustafayez Art Museum in Baku. "I changed the colors and attempted to make the colors look a bit faded to signify age." Hooked by Shirley Chaiken. New Hampshire. 2004. 22" x 24.5" *Courtesy of Shirley Chaiken.*

Petite "Persian Garden." A very successful first hooking project. Designed by Pearl McGown. W. Cushing and Company pattern. Hooked by Pat Cardin. Georgia. 2005. 15" x 23.5". *Courtesy of Pat Cardin.*

"Gabbea," invites us to the land of camels. Hooked with woolen yarns, the story rug is framed by a traditional Azeri-style border. Designed by Jane McGown Flynn. House of Price / Charco pattern. Hooked by Shirley S. Lothrop. Maine. 1999. 54" x 34". *Courtesy of Shirley S. Lothrop.*

Images of the modern Western world, farms, tractor, school bus, and the American flag, are conveyed in the style reminiscent of Eastern storytelling tribal rugs. "East Meets West" is the companion piece to the aforementioned "Gabbea." Hooked with woolen yarns. Designed by Jane McGown Flynn. House of Price / Charco pattern. Hooked by Shirley S. Lothrop. Maine 2000. 58" x 44". *Courtesy of Shirley S. Lothrop.*

African and Afro-American Hooked Art

Rug hookers embrace an allegiance to traditions, cultures, and ideals of both Africa and North America.

After having lost her only son, Gaylord, in a pool accident, Carol Ann Pinkins turned to rug hooking to "heal and lessen the pain." A few months after the tragic incident she completed "Cotton Picking" on what would have been his thirty-fifth birthday. "Cotton Picking." Pris Buttler Rug Designs pattern. Hooked by Carol Ann Pinkins. California. 2002. 23.5" x 55.5". *Courtesy of Carol Ann Pinkins.*

One year and five days after the death of her own son, Carol Ann Pinkins' nephew, whom she helped raise, died in a car crash. Again she turned to rug hooking to relieve the pain and completed "Family Outing" a month before Duncan Gibson's thirty-fifth birthday. Her hooked tribute depicts a mother, baby, and four children parading in front of an array of sunflowers. Inspired by the Julia Cairns 2003 Celebration Calendar and adapted with permission of the artist. "Family Outing." Julia Cairns. Hooked by Carol Ann Pinkins. California. 2003. 44" x 60". *Courtesy of Carol Ann Pinkins.*

Karen Detrick's "Rug Hookers On the Farm" was adapted from Pris Buttler's "Freedom Quilt" pattern. "The quilt makers became rug hookers, the original hound dog was reborn as the family Airedale, Bailey, and the background was transformed into the rolling hills of Perry County, Ohio." Pris Buttler Rug Designs pattern. Hooked by Karen Detrick. Ohio. 2004. 22" x 30". *Courtesy of Karen Detrick.*

Beset with personal tragedy, Carol Ann Pinkins recalls happier times. "Mother Love," portrays an intimate vignette. Children and a festively dressed mother form bold silhouettes against lush vegetation and fertile earth. A lively orange border frames the scene. Inspired by the Julia Cairns 2004 Celebration Calendar and adapted with permission of the artist. "Mother Love." Julia Cairns. Hooked by Carol Ann Pinkins. California. 2004. 52.5" x 41". *Courtesy of Carol Ann Pinkins.*

Hooked Postcards—Wish You Were Here

As The Beatles once immortalized in song, "There are places I'll remember all my life though some have changed..." Rug makers pay tribute to those special places using their hearts, hand, and hook.

Right:
Halfway through their "Trip West," Beverly Osgood's husband forgot to reload the camera. With hook in hand, Beverly saved the memories and fashioned a rug depicting Niagara Falls, the Grand Hotel, Yellowstone, her brother-in-law's house, the Ennis Rodeo, Jackson Hole, the Great Plains, parasailing in Wisconsin, and a wedding in New York. Crisscrossing highways and familiar roadside signs frame the hooked travel log. Designed and hooked by Beverly Osgood. Connecticut. 2002. 46" x 66". *Courtesy of Beverly Osgood.*

A view from Sausalito, California overlooking San Francisco Bay, where the hooking artist's daughter, Lauren, and her cat, Kayla, lived for thirteen years. "Kayla's World." Designed and hooked by Judy Fresk. Connecticut. 1999. 25" x 41". *Courtesy of Judy Fresk.*

Shards of light filter through California's majestic giants. "Sequoia Sunrise." Designed and hooked by Beth Kempf. Connecticut. 2001. 46.5" x 35". *Courtesy of Beth Kempf.*

"True to his native Hopi ancestors, Cabot Yerxa (1882-1965) hand-built his adobe pueblo in Desert Hot Springs, California. Working in the desert for thirty years, carrying water seven miles from the railroad station, Yerxa built his Hopi-style tribute four stories high with 150 windows and 65 doors. Today it is a museum filled with Native American pottery and his oil paintings." "Yerxa's Adobe House." Adapted from a San Gabriel Tribune photograph. Made into a pattern by Jane Olson. Hooked by Norma Piper. California. 2003. 12" x 18". *Courtesy of Norma Piper.*

"Springdale" chronicles happy times spent with family near Spokane, Washington. Adapted from a 1977 drawing by Erma Latham Watrous, the hooking artist's mother. Hooked by Wilma Watrous Mewes. Oregon. 2001. 19" x 30". Courtesy of *Wilma Watrous Mewes*.

When her daughter's much desired trip to Hawaii didn't materialize because of financial reasons, Kathy Stephens thought the least she could do was to hook her this postcard image of the island paradise. "Joyful Joyful." Designed and hooked by Kathy T. Stephens. Montana. 2004. 25" x 37". *Courtesy of Kathy T. Stephens.*

"View from my Window—the Three Sisters." "On a spring day, right after a shower, the sky had dark clouds with the sun shining through on the Middle and South Sisters. The North Sister looked darker. Pictured in the foreground are the red cinders from volcanic ash appearing much more colorful when wet. The big lone tree is a juniper—symbolic of the high desert in Central Oregon." Designed and hooked by Jean Zehr. Oregon. 2004. 26" x 49". *Courtesy of Jean Zehr.*

"Mom's Childhood Home—Madison County, Iowa." The century old farm is located not far from the house used in the filming of *The Bridges of Madison County*. Adapted from photographs. Made into a pattern by Jane Olson. Hooked by Norma Gillette. Oregon. 2002. 22" x 31". *Courtesy of Norma Gillette.*

A serene and peaceful glimpse of the "Pond on Ancient Oak Lane, St Charles, Illinois." Designed and hooked by Suzanne S. Hamer. Illinois. 2000. 10" x 12". *Courtesy of Suzanne S. Hamer.*

"Lake Pend Oreille." "Northern Idaho must be one of the most beautiful places I have seen. Several family members were mountain climbing when we encountered this beautiful view." Adapted from a photograph with added moose and flowers. Designed and hooked by Sally D'Albora. Maryland. 1998. 23" x 37". *Courtesy of Sally D'Albora.*

Far Right:
"Having lived near the Chesapeake Bay all my life I'm intrigued by the beautiful wildlife it harbors." "Chesapeake Marsh II: Red Winged Blackbirds." Designed and hooked by Sally D'Albora. Maryland. 2001. 35" x 26". *Courtesy of Sally D'Albora.*

Right:
Detail of "Chesapeake Marsh II: Red Winged Blackbirds." *Courtesy of Sally D'Albora.*

"New Life." "This piece was conceived to continue the [aforementioned] Chesapeake Bay series. The design is original but not terribly accurate—since the female turtle will deposit her eggs up to a year before they will hatch. But to embellish the work, I decided to show the babies, all seven of them, struggling to live. As you can see, only one makes it." Designed and hooked by Sally D'Albora. Maryland. 2002. 40" x 37". *Courtesy of Sally D'Albora.*

The historic "Toll House" of Silver Springs, Maryland, served up meals and collected tolls from those traveling on the Washington-Ashton-Colesville Turnpike, a main route for bringing goods into the city. Adapted from recent and vintage photographs. Hooked by Sarah Province. Maryland. 2003. 12" x 18". *Courtesy of Sarah Province.*

Detail of "New Life." *Courtesy of Sally D'Albora.*

Vermont's "March Madness." "My husband Michael deserved a rug all his own because he has been so supportive of my hooking passion. His rite of spring, along with the basketball playoffs, is sugaring. It is his sign that winter is on the way out." Designed and hooked by Susan Mackey. Vermont. 2002. 26" x 29". *Courtesy of Susan Mackey.*

"Cal's Porch." Even a president needs to sit, rock, and watch the world go by. Adapted from a photograph of Calvin Coolidge's Vermont home. Hooked by Nancy Coates. Oregon. 1996. 20.5" x 30". *Courtesy of Nancy Coates.*

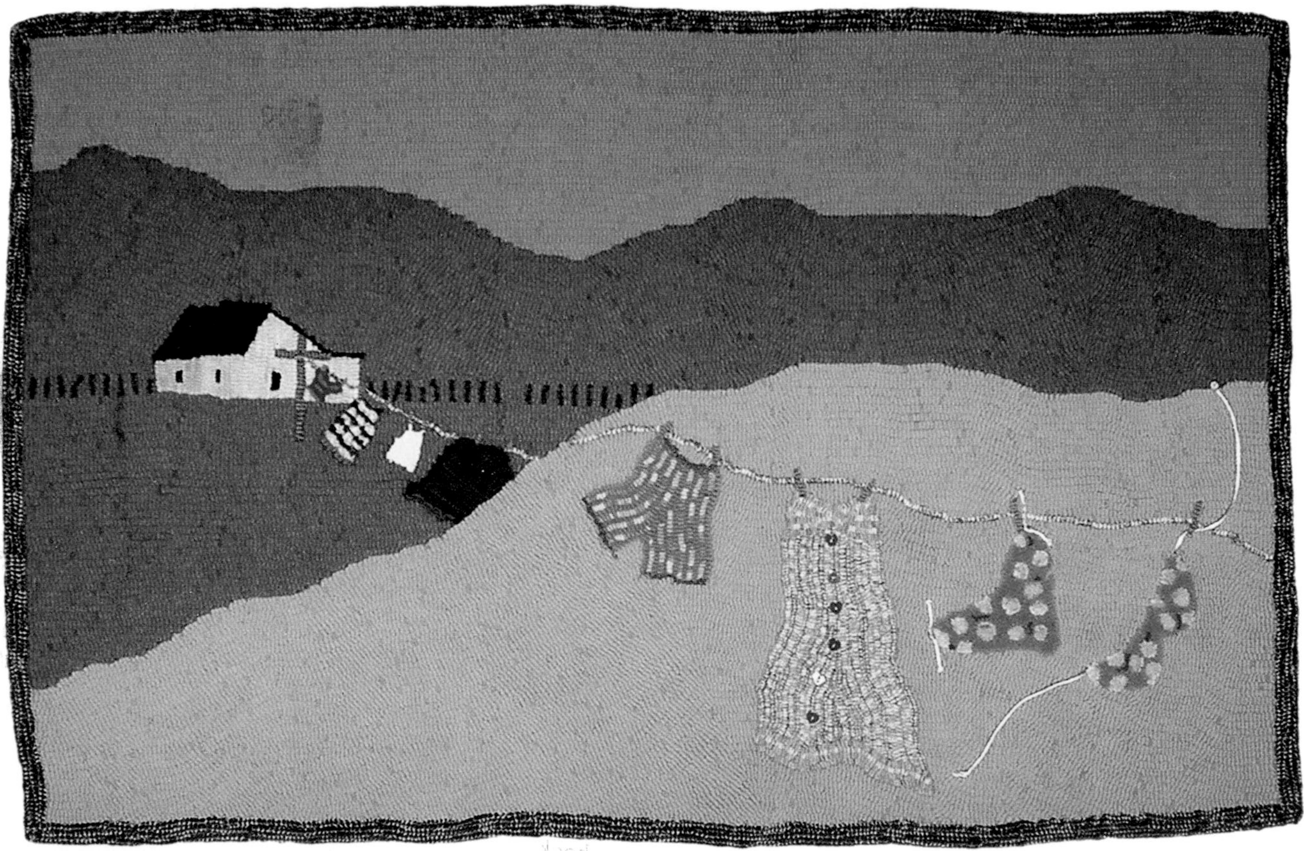

"I love seeing laundry hanging outdoors, sometimes framed by beautiful countryside or sometimes providing the spark of color amidst the cold gray urban landscape." Button and yarn embellishments were added to the hooked clothing. "Laundry Day." Designed and hooked by Polly Alexander. Vermont. 28" x 44". *Courtesy of Polly Alexander.*

"Vermont." "I hooked this rug for my daughter with the words 'sunshine' and 'happiness' on it. The words are from a song I share with her." Designed and hooked by Joan Hebert. Vermont. 2003. 27" x 37". *Courtesy of Joan Hebert.*

"The View from Middle Mountain." "I live on an island in the Penobscot Bay with many beautiful vistas. We often walk our dogs in the Middle Mountain Park, one of the highest points on the island, where, in the fall, the huckleberry bushes turn to blazing oranges and reds. This rug was inspired by the view from Maine's Middle Mountain across Penobscot Bay to the Camden Hills." Designed and hooked by Carol Morris Petillo. Maine. 2004. 32" x 35". *Courtesy of Carol Morris Petillo.*

Left:
A postcard view of "The Commons of Little Compton," the hooking artist's Rhode Island hometown. Designed and hooked by Pam Evans. Rhode Island. 2005. 48.5" x 31.5". *Courtesy of Pam Evans.*

It's nice to "Summer in Maine" on Sawyer's Island. Designed and hooked by Debbie Torre. Rhode Island. 2003. 39" x 39". *Courtesy of Debbie Torre.*

A hooked map of the "USA." Heirloom Rug pattern. Hooked by Shirley S. Lothrop. Maine. 1998. 44" x 66". *Courtesy of Shirley S. Lothrop.*

I first saw "Medicine Lake" in Canada in 1998. My husband was driving and I asked him to stop. The color of the lake was so beautiful that I knew I wanted to make a rug like it." Designed and hooked by Cosette Allen. Vermont. 2004. 25" x 41". *Courtesy of Cosette Allen.*

"The Animals are Out." A Canadian maritime summer scene, complete with a roof ladder to remind us that winter is not far off. Deanne Fitzpatrick pattern. Hooked by Barbara Holt Hussey. New Hampshire. 2001. 21" x 34". *Courtesy of Barbara Holt Hussey.*

Pots of bright flowers brighten a corner of "Tuscany." Adapted from a photo postcard. Hooked by Theresa Strack. New Hampshire. 2004. 16" x 12". *Courtesy of Theresa Strack.*

"Streets of Bamburg." "While visiting Germany, I traveled to several old cities and this is an example of one of the more interesting ones." Designed and hooked by Theresa Strack. New Hampshire. 2000. 18" x 12". *Courtesy of Theresa Strack.*

Recalling times spent with family on a island in the Bahamas. "Bradford." Lib Callaway pattern / Hook Nook. Hooked by Rose M. Bradfield. Rhode Island. 2005. 20" x 32". *Courtesy of Rose M. Bradfield.*

"Tour de McAleer." "My mother, sibling, assorted spouses, and I took a bike tour of the Loire Valley in the fall of 1995. The rug depicts one of the many fascinating villages we biked by. It is the view above the town looking down from the chateau in Amboise, France. The border includes a bike for each family member on the trip and the field after field of sunflowers we passed along the way." Designed and hooked by Carol McAleer Munson. Vermont. 1996. 28" x 33". *Courtesy of Carol McAleer Munson.*

Below:
"'Waiting for My Master' was adapted from a photograph that I took on a trip to the Provence region in France. The little white dog was just sitting in front of this old weathered blue building, waiting for someone to come. To me, this told a story and made a great photograph." Hooked by Nancy Coates. Oregon. 2002. 22" x 31". *Courtesy of Nancy Coates.*

Tomatoes, Eggplants, and Squash

Hooked produce takes a stand. Often overlooked because of popular motifs featuring apples, pears, grapes, and other favorite fruits, less glamourous garden delicacies such as tomatoes, eggplant, and squash are suddenly appearing on more and more hooked rugs. Are peaches passé? Hooked pumpkin fans hope so.

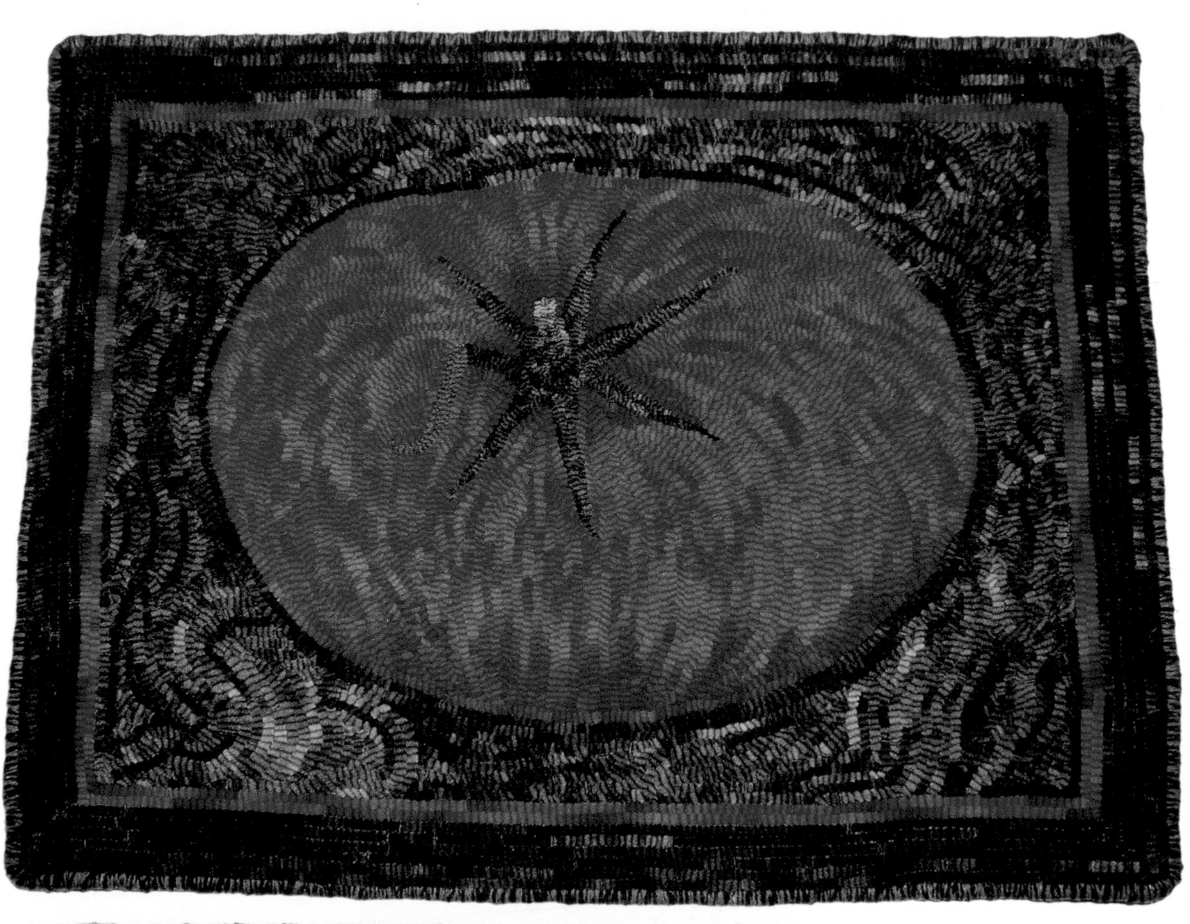

What a "Tomato!" After seeing an artist paint large fruit, Jean Zehr picked up her hook and paid tribute to this versatile queen of the backyard gardens. Designed and hooked by Jean Zehr. Oregon. 2004. 21.5" x 28". *Courtesy of Jean Zehr.*

"Pumpkin Patch." "This rug has my favorite background—deep purples mixed in with black and other darks. It really makes the orange shades of the pumpkins pop out." Designed and hooked by Janine Williams. Texas. 2004. 16" x 22.5". *Courtesy of Janine Williams.*

Mix together eggplants, tomatoes, and a series of delightful borders and what do you get? "Ratatouille." Designed and hooked by Judy Fresk. Connecticut. 32" x 34". *Courtesy of Judy Fresk.*

A perfect "Big Pumpkin" hooked in earthy colors of fall. Curlicue tendrils, vines, and stem echo the roundness of the hooked squash. Designed by Matt Moore. Hooked by Polly Reinhart. Pennsylvania. 2000. 25" x 28". *Courtesy of Polly Reinhart.*

Hooked pillows are comforting reminders of autumn's glorious pumpkin colors. "My grandmother was the first rug hooker in our family. She told me, 'Never throw away a piece of wool.'" After hooking "Pumpkin Pillow," the leftovers were used to fashion "Fall Leaf Pillow." Tiny clipped off ends were used to stuff both. Both designed and hooked by Karen Cooper. New Hampshire. "Fall Leaf Pillow." 1999. 13" x 13". "Pumpkin Pillow." 1996. 16" x 13". *Courtesy of Karen Cooper.*

Continuing a family tradition, Corinne Goss Carignan hooked the blue Hubbard of "3 Pumpkins and a Blue Hubbard Squash" from vintage woolen fabrics that once belonged to her paternal grandmother. The resourceful "Grammy Goss," born in 1892 and twice widowed, hooked and sold rugs to support her family. Modern additions to the rug included as is and hand-dyed wools. Designed and hooked by Corinne A. Goss Carignan. Maine. 2004. 25.5" x 33.5". *Courtesy of Corinne A. Goss Carignan.*

"Pumpkins on the Fence;" a perfect backdrop for supporting vines and highlighting a squash trio. Designed and hooked by Sharon Saknit. California. 2003. 22" x 17". *Courtesy of Sharon Saknit.*

Rebecca Erb—Sinking Spring, Pennsylvania

Rebecca Erb, rug hooking artist, teacher, and entrepreneur, has an eye for wool. "The Wool Studio," her mail order business, offers a treasure trove of hooking wools, including desirable plaids, checks, herringbones, and so much more. In her spare time, Rebecca designs and creates hooked rugs for family and friends—rugs that become cherished heirlooms.

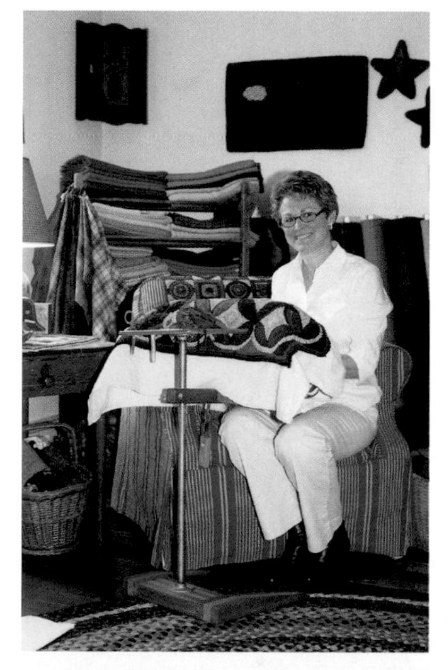

Rebecca Erb poised at her rug hooking frame. *Courtesy of Rebecca Erb.*

Scores of circles crowd around a hooked advertisement proclaiming "Wool for Sale." A lamb's tongue border adds a decorative touch and recalls early penny rugs. Designed by Matt Moore. Hooked by Rebecca Erb. Pennsylvania. 2001. 14" x 23". *Courtesy of Rebecca Erb.*

"Geometric" triple play. Stars join circles, squares, and rectangles. Hooked with all as is earthy tone woolen fabrics. Adapted from a quilt pattern. Designed and hooked by Rebecca Erb. Pennsylvania. 2004. 18" x 42". *Courtesy of Rebecca Erb.*

"Studio Angel." A primitive image, hooked with a bit of whimsy, guides us through the night. Designed and hooked by Rebecca Erb. Pennsylvania. 1997. 30" x 60". *Courtesy of Rebecca Erb.*

A guardian angel tends a crewel-like bouquet hooked in celebration of "A Love for All Seasons." Contouring lines of closely related background colors add interest to the cherished remembrance of a daughter's wedding. Designed and hooked by Rebecca Erb. Pennsylvania. 1997. 33" x 52". *Courtesy of Rebecca Erb.*

"Pearl, May, and Laverne." A trio of "funky" chickens named for three sisters. Decorative circles dance inside and outside a scalloped line border. Designed by son-in-law Matt Moore for Rebecca's birthday. Hooked by Rebecca Erb. Pennsylvania. 1999. 24" x 34". *Courtesy of Rebecca Erb.*

Hooked before the arrival of a first grandchild. "Mr. and Mrs. Bunny and Baby" walk into a glorious, color filled sunset. Adapted from a one-inch sized illustration found in an antique children's book. Hooked by Rebecca Erb. Pennsylvania 1999. 22" x 26". *Courtesy of Rebecca Erb.*

A hooked collage of childhood "Nursery Rhymes" fashioned for first granddaughter, Lydia. Designed by Matt Moore and Rebecca Erb. Hooked by Rebecca Erb. Pennsylvania. 2003. 31" x 30". *Courtesy of Rebecca Erb.*

This group of ladies originally signed up for a 5-week beginner's rug hooking class in 1999. They have been coming once a week to see Rebecca Erb (far right) ever since. "They no longer learn from me, but we learn from one another." Each was given the same pattern to hook. You can see the greatly varied results. *Courtesy of Rebecca Erb.*

Fruit

Fruit has always been a favorite subject for rug makers to hook. The varieties are countless, the colors delectable, and the subject matter pleasing to all.

Artist Fiona Cooper Fenwick put down her paint brush and picked up a hook. "The Three Pears" was adapted from one of her pastel paintings. "I took a workshop with Rae Harrell [Vermont rug hooking artist and teacher] and she encouraged me to take the leap into an original design. We dyed most of the wool in the workshop and I began to paint with wool. It became more than I could have hoped for, both visually and personally." "The Three Pears." Designed and hooked by Fiona Cooper Fenwick. Vermont. 2004. 24" x 27.5". *Courtesy of Fiona Cooper Fenwick.*

ATHA
NEWSLETTER
A Publication
of the Association
of Traditional Hooking Artists

p. 10 'Ceres Rug'
Hooked by Sharon Garland
Designed by Pearl K. McGown
48" x 68"

VOL. 20, NO. 143
October / November 2003

Cornucopias and baskets, overflowing with fruit, join a finely shaded leaf scroll to frame a central fruited medallion. This exceptional hooked rug graced the cover of ATHA's (Association of Traditional Hooking Artists) October/November 2003 newsletter. "Ceres." Designed by Pearl McGown. W. Cushing and Company pattern. Hooked by Sharon Garland. Oregon. 2000. 73" x 47". *Courtesy of Sharon Garland and ATHA – Association of Traditional Hooking Artists.*

Buzzing above "Golden Fruit." A lush array of pumpkin, fruit, and foliage set against a dark background. Designed by Joan Moshimer. W. Cushing and Company pattern. Hooked by Joan Mohrmann. New York. 2002. 25" x 40". *Courtesy of Joan Mohrmann.*

Another version of aforementioned "Golden Fruit" with a light background and added outer border. Designed by Joan Moshimer. W. Cushing and Company pattern. Hooked by Ruthann Boynton. Connecticut. 2004. 25" x 41". *Courtesy of Ruthann Boynton.*

"Helen's Pants." "It was at Dexter's Inn, in New Hampshire, at the McGown [rug hooking] School that I saw Helen Dyement wearing polyester pants that looked so good I asked her to give them to me if she ever tired of them. Lo and behold, she mailed them to me. Jane Olson [California rug hooking artist, designer, and teacher] drew the pattern for me and taught me how to hook fruit from this. I did most of the dyeing and learned from that too." Rug hookers are notorious for scouting out clothing that can be used for future projects. Most prefer to hook with woolen fabric, but Susan Andreson, willing to take chances, experimented with polyester. Now renamed "Fruit Runner." Jane Olson pattern. Hooked by Susan Andreson. California. 1998. 12" x 18". *Courtesy of Susan Andreson.*

Forest pine cones join a garden's bounty. The pattern for this rug was purchased by Carol White in the early 1970s but never hooked. Years later, her friend Donna Armour picked up a hook and took on the project. "Fruit and Pine Cones—Fireside Half Rug." Harry M. Fraser Company pattern. Hooked by Donna Armour. Rhode Island. 2002. 25.5" x 43". *Courtesy of Donna M. Armour.*

Right:
Four pineapples, each sporting a different patterned rind, fill decorative quadrants of this quilt influenced design. "Crossed Pineapples." Vermont Folk Rugs pattern. Hooked by Davey DeGraff. Vermont. 2002. 52" x 52". *Courtesy of Davey DeGraff.*

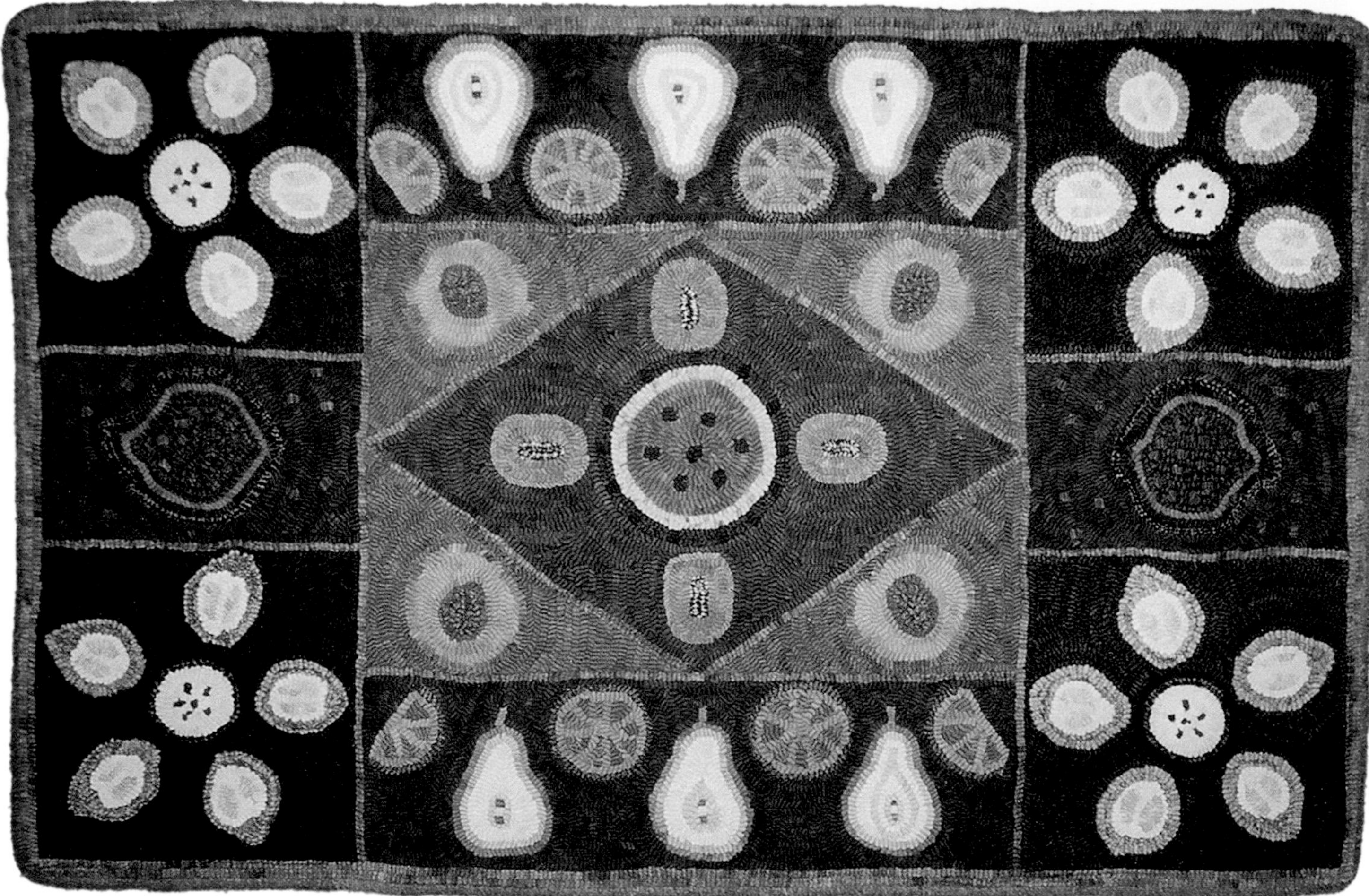

"Sliced Fruit." A fresh look at summer produce. "It was fun to try to hook the fruit in as realistic colors as possible and yet keep it 'folky' and old looking." Vermont Folk Rugs pattern. Hooked by Davey DeGraff. Vermont. 1997. 27" x 41". *Courtesy of Davey DeGraff.*

A tiny image found on an old oven mitt was the inspiration for "Floating Pine-apples." Shades of purple and gold meld. Designed and hooked by Kathy T. Stephens. Montana. 2005. 24" x 36". *Courtesy of Kathy T. Stephens.*

Fanciful flowers pair off with an exotic fruit. Diamond motifs from the pineapple's prickly rind join a meandering leafy vine to form this rug's unique outer border. "Primitive Floral." Beverly Conway Designs. Hooked by Diane Burgess. Vermont. 2000. 24" x 48". *Courtesy of Diane Burgess.*

Multiple borders protect cherished "Fruit Blocks." "This is my very favorite rug, as it was the last rug hooked under the instruction of my teacher/mentor—Janet Dobson of Hope Valley, Rhode Island. She passed away shortly after we finished the six blocks. I continued to design the next three borders. I think she would have approved and maybe even liked it. I'll always think of her and her devotion to the rug hooking world and the people in it when I look at this piece." Designed by Janet Dobson and Andrea Scott Trout. Hooked by Andrea Scott Trout. Rhode Island. 1996–1997. 32" x 44". *Courtesy of Andrea Scott Trout.*

"This was my first attempt at fruit, canned no less! Keeping the individual fruits well defined was a challenge. Following the reds and yellows of the chili peppers is like following an M.C. Escher print. Another challenge was the color of the water in each jar. I think I'll stick to animals." "Canning Jars." Designed by Mary Ellen Wolff. Hooked by Susan Naples. California. 2004. 17" x 28". *Courtesy of Susan Naples*.

Ripe fruit combines with blossoms, buds, and foliage to compose a decorative spray. Used as a piano bench cover. "Bountiful Harvest." Designed and hooked by Karen Goulart. Rhode Island. 2004. 14.5" x 29.5". *Courtesy of Karen Goulart*.

A petit-point still life of fruit plus a pattern from a wood carving manual served as inspiration for this rug hooker. "Summer Harvest Still Life." Designed and hooked by Janice M. Lacey. New Hampshire. 2003. 27" x 47". *Courtesy of Janice M. Lacey*.

Octagonal medallions hold eight different fruit studies. A lively outer border offers a complementary finishing touch. "Fruit Print Ensemble." Designed by Pearl McGown. W. Cushing and Company pattern. Hooked by Joan Mohrmann. New York. 1997. 42" x 79". *Courtesy of Joan Mohrmann*.

Abstract Hooking

"Abstract: having only intrinsic form with little or no attempt at pictorial representation" is one of the meanings the *Merriam Webster's Collegiate Dictionary* attaches to the word. Rug makers create their own abstract interpretations by letting their hooks and imaginations wander.

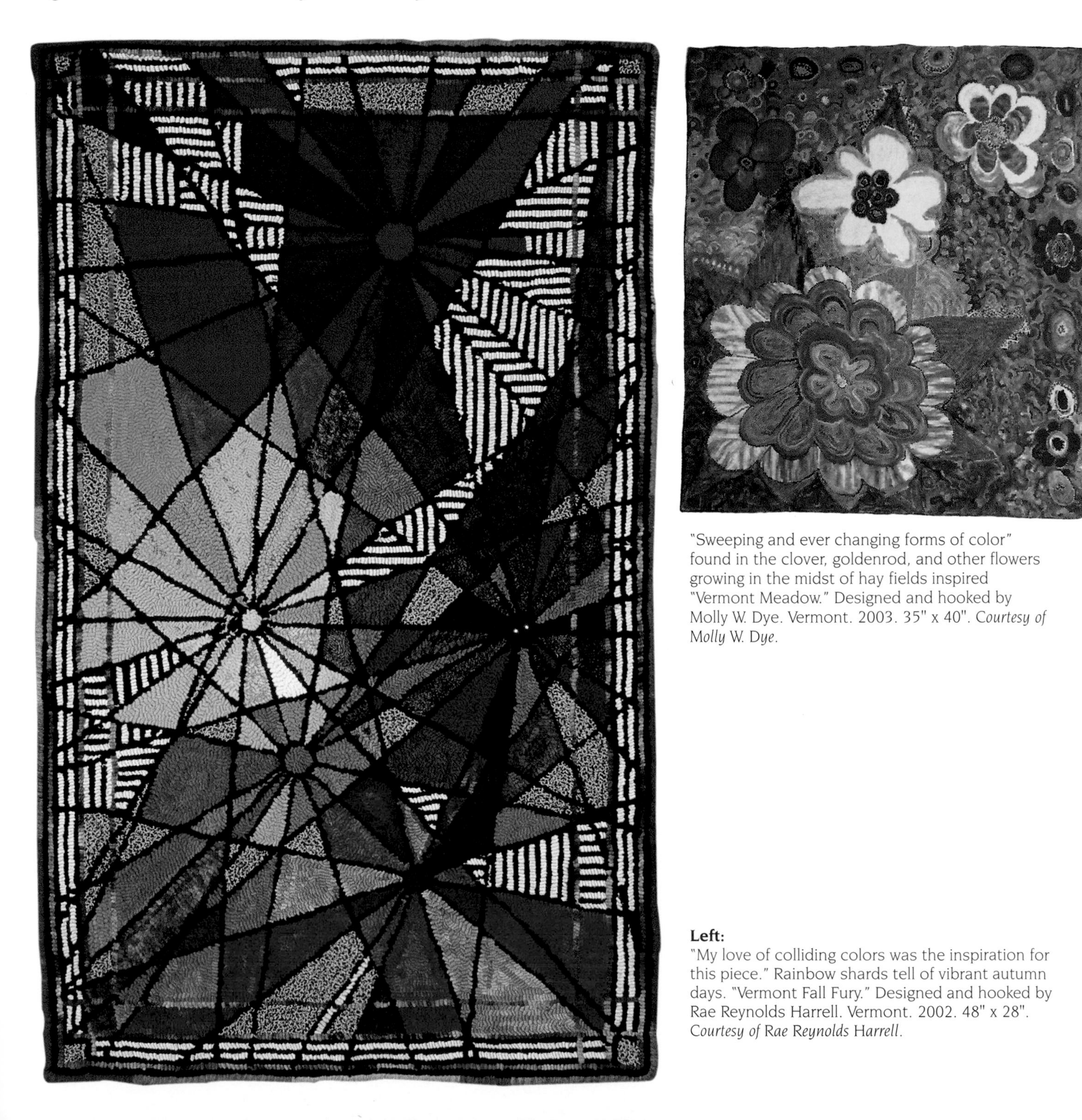

"Sweeping and ever changing forms of color" found in the clover, goldenrod, and other flowers growing in the midst of hay fields inspired "Vermont Meadow." Designed and hooked by Molly W. Dye. Vermont. 2003. 35" x 40". *Courtesy of Molly W. Dye.*

Left:
"My love of colliding colors was the inspiration for this piece." Rainbow shards tell of vibrant autumn days. "Vermont Fall Fury." Designed and hooked by Rae Reynolds Harrell. Vermont. 2002. 48" x 28". *Courtesy of Rae Reynolds Harrell.*

Lively bursts of floral colors. "My Impression of My Spring Garden." Designed and hooked by Susan Andreson. California. 2004. 10" x 16". *Courtesy of Susan Andreson.*

An abstract remembrance. "This rug was a hooking journal for the month of September 2004. The backing was divided into thirty sections and every day I hooked the things I saw around me: grapevines, leaves, pears, butterflies, Kilim rugs, woven shawls, whatever I felt like hooking each day." "September Play." Designed and hooked by Judith Dallegret. Quebec, Canada. 2004. 30" x 55". *Courtesy of Judith Dallegret.*

Abstract flowers within a checkered diamond frame dance on polychrome waves of color. "Untitled." Designed and hooked by Mary Anne Wise. Wisconsin. 2003. 32" x 38". *Courtesy of Mary Anne Wise.*

Abstract forms from outer space. "Cosmic." Designed and hooked by Suzan Farrens. California. 2002. 29" x 41". *Courtesy of Suzan Farrens.*

"Color Study." A transitional field, moving from dark to light, serves as a backdrop for meandering blue lines contained within a framework of like color. Designed and hooked by Suzan Farrens. California. 2004. 72" x 12". *Courtesy of Suzan Farrens.*

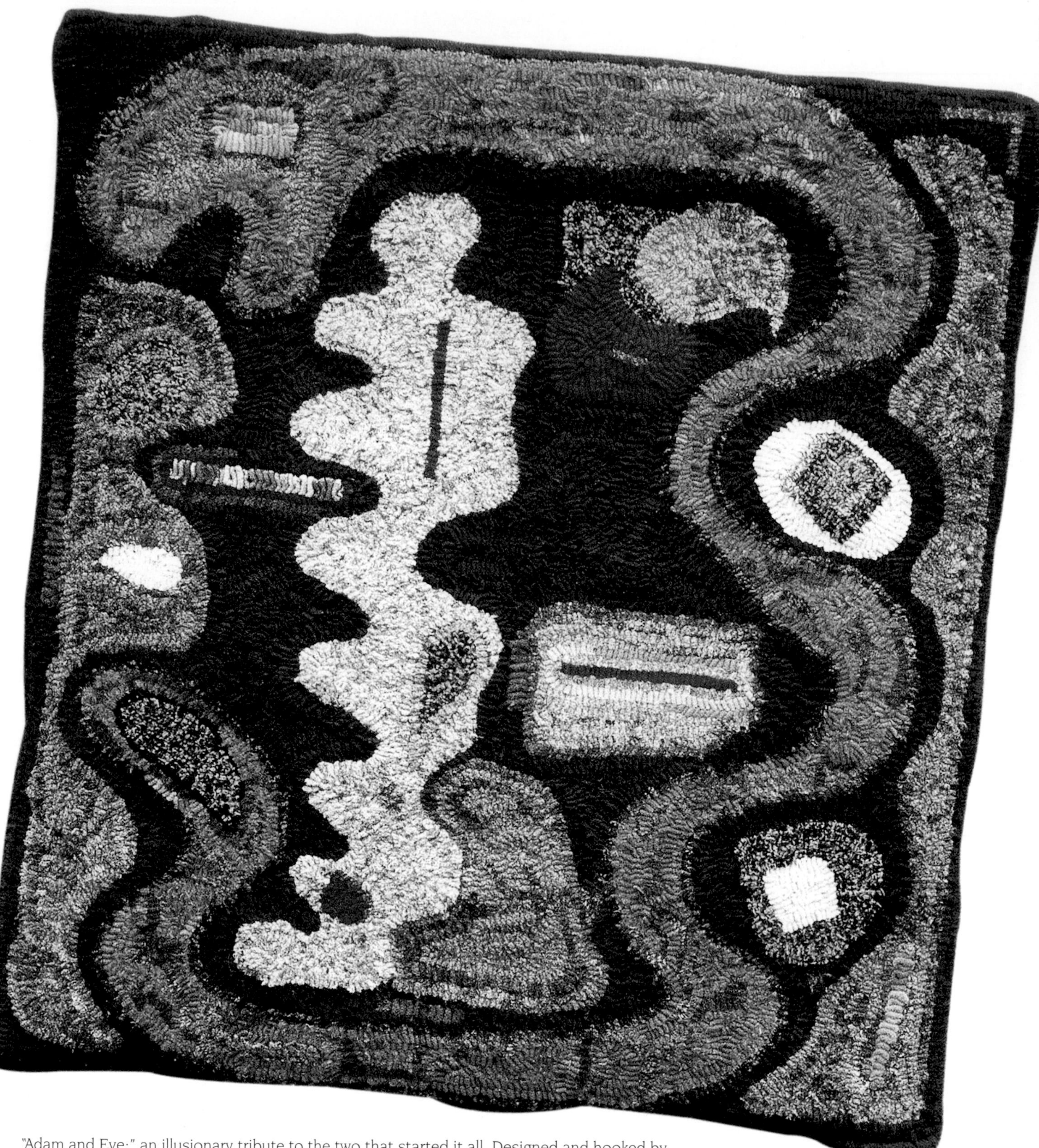

"Adam and Eve;" an illusionary tribute to the two that started it all. Designed and hooked by Susan Feller. West Virginia. 2002. 24" x 23". *Courtesy of Susan Feller - Ruckman Mill Farm.*

Dogs

Dogs…many a rug hooker's best friend.

English painter George Stubbs (1724-1806) would be pleased with this hooked likeness of his famous canines. "Stubbs Dogs." Designed by Joan Moshimer. W. Cushing and Company pattern. Hooked by Carole Beeson. Missouri. 2003. 22" x 48". *Courtesy of Carole Beeson.*

Carole Beeson's "Sheep Dog" possesses a painterly quality found in century old portraits. Margaret Hunt Masters pattern. Prairie Craft House. Hooked by Carole Beeson. Missouri. 2005. 42" x 52. *Courtesy of Carole Beeson.*

"Kilian," the world traveling golden retriever, became part of the Miller family while they were stationed in Bamberg, Germany. His hooked portrait was started upon return to the United States. Adapted from a photograph. Made into a pattern by Elizabeth Black. Hooked by Tricia Tague Miller. New Hampshire. 1996. 21" x 33". *Courtesy of Tricia Tague Miller.*

"Love of Pugs." "We had both these pugs since they were pups. They gave us two litters of pups and lots of joy for thirteen years. Both dogs are gone now and I wanted their spirits to live on. So I decided to hook a rug featuring them." Duke and Neeka are framed by their favorite treats. Designed and hooked by Alitza Wildes. Maine. 2004. 25" x 36.5". *Courtesy of Alitza Wildes.*

Details from "Love of Pugs." *Courtesy of* Alitza Wildes.

"As we all know, when a dog moves into your house, it moves into your heart as well. 'Our Girl,' Jazz, lived with us for seven years and the love between her and my husband was noteworthy. I decided to do this hooking for him as a Christmas present. It was a perfect gift as she soon left us." Designed and hooked by Sally D'Albora. Maryland. 2002. 28" x 52". *Courtesy of Sally D'Albora.*

Detail of "Our Girl." *Courtesy of Sally D'Albora.*

Birch leaves fall as a beloved family pet finds his way home. As a gift to her parents, Jennifer Manuell hooked this rug to commemorate a truly "Top Dog." Designed and hooked by Jennifer Manuell. Ontario, Canada. 2000. 25" x 34.5" *Courtesy of Jennifer Manuell.*

Saved from the pound when he was just a round ball of fur, Panda is now in dog paradise living with rug hooking artist Ramona Maddox and her husband Owen. He spends his days by their pool playing with toys. "Panda on Point." Adapted from a photograph. Made into a pattern by Designs by Debbie. Hooked by Ramona Maddox. Tennessee. 2005. 25" x 50". *Courtesy of Ramona Maddox.*

Double the trouble. Double the fun. "My Two Corgis." Adapted from a photograph. Hooked by Fran Oken. Vermont. 2002. 16" x 23". *Courtesy of Fran Oken.*

"Our Family" captures images of Shelties (left to right) Samantha Rose, Casey, Kipp and Nate—each of whom was dearly loved. Daylily, spiderwort, and blue flag iris envelop the furry four. Designed by Ann Winterling. Hooked by Karen Sullivan. Maine. 2005. 20" x 34". *Courtesy of Karen Sullivan.*

"Ajax and Jettson In Dream Land." "The feisty dachshund and the easy going 80-pound golden retriever were generally known as the odd couple." Designed and hooked by Sue Lawler. Vermont. 2000. 20" x 35". *Courtesy of Sue Lawler.*

Who could resist the likes of "Bandit"? Nancy Coates hooked this portrait of a truly grateful dog after Bandit was rescued by Nancy's son and his wife. Adapted from a photograph and drawn as a pattern by Jane Olson. Hooked by Nancy Coates. Oregon. 2002. 15.5" x 13". *Courtesy of Nancy Coates.*

"Buffy" sports a colorful bandana and a mischievous look. Designed and hooked by Elizabeth Morgan. Vermont. 2002. 25.5" x 21". *Courtesy of Elizabeth Morgan.*

A pillow portraiture of "Shaggy." Designed by Jane McGown Flynn. House of Price / Charco pattern. Hooked by Suzanne S. Hamer. Illinois. 2003. 17" x 13". *Courtesy of Suzanne S. Hamer.*

A camera shy "Mittens" wouldn't let Lois Egenes take her photograph but was agreeable to having her portrait hooked. Designed and hooked Lois Egenes. Iowa. 2003. 14" x 12". *Courtesy of Lois Egenes.*

To the American Kennel Club she is registered as Tilly's Springtime Bonanza but to Trish Becker her canine companion is Bonnie. The frisky Labrador retriever is framed by orange tulips from the garden where she loves to play. "Bonnie in Tulips." Designed and hooked by Trish Becker. 2004. 25" x 27". *Courtesy of Trish Becker–The Woolery, Inc.*

"My Jane." Rug hooker Jean Johnson fell in love with Jane, her daughter's Jack Russell terrier. Upon completion of this hooked portrait, Jean's husband gave her Chloe, a Jack Russell of her own. As dear as Chloe is, "there will never be another Jane." Designed by Julie Ludke. Hooked by Jean Johnson. Michigan. 2000. 25" x 36". *Courtesy of Jean Johnson.*

Detail of "My Jane." *Courtesy of Jean Johnson.*

"Patches" likes to "monkey" around. Adapted from a photograph and drawn as a pattern by Nancy Scharf. Hooked by Joan Watterson. Oregon. 2004. 17" x 17". *Courtesy of Joan Watterson.*

"Paw Prints on My Heart." "Fritz came to me as a rescued stray in October 1991. Together, we traveled through thirteen years of life. The rug shows a whimsical face, a doghouse, and toys surrounding him. There is the ever-important food dish!" Designed and hooked by Karen Quigley. Vermont. 2002. 38" x 32". *Courtesy of Karen Quigley.*

"Sage Dog" wears a heart and halo. Adapted from a water color image by Maren Spitta McMillan. Hooked by Patsy Spitta. California. 2002. 33" x 38". *Courtesy of Patsy Spitta.*

A rug for hooked for "Taffy." "She was my mother's beloved cocker spaniel, who died a number of years ago but has always remained in a loving and honored place in her heart—thus the hearts and stars in the corners." Designed and hooked by Nancy L. Brown. New Hampshire. 1997. 18" x 26". *Courtesy of* Nancy L. Brown.

Her love for Scottish terriers prompted hooking artist Andrea Scott Trout to create this tribute to her loyal, loving watch dogs. Plaid woolen fabric was used to hook the red and black border. "Scottie Plaid." Designed by Kathy Thorton. Hooked by Andrea Scott Trout. Rhode Island. 2001. 23" x 45". *Courtesy of Andrea Scott Trout.*

A folk art rendition of beloved pets, George, Jesse, and Willow—the trio that often gets into trouble. "In the Dog House." Vermont Folk Rugs pattern. Hooked by Davey DeGraff. Vermont. 2002. 22" x 40". *Courtesy of Davey DeGraff.*

Home is Where the Hook Is

There is no place like home. Rug makers often pick up their hooks and portray where their heart is.

Vibrant blossoms welcome all. Memories of the charming "Lake Lanier House," designed by the hooking artist's husband and now sold, are preserved in this delightful hooked scene. Designed by the artist's daughter, Lisa Carey VanMeter. Hooked by Joyce B. Carey. Georgia. 2002. 30" x 50". *Courtesy of Joyce B. Carey.*

The O'Connor home is hooked with gardens a bit more lush and vibrant than reality. Swirling striated skies create movement and light up "My Ideal." Designed and hooked by Mary Lee O'Connor. New York. 2002. 16" x 78". *Courtesy Mary Lee O'Connor.*

Pictured is Davey DeGraff's Vermont home on Lake Iroquois. The "How Dear to My Heart" verse that partially frames the rug was taken from a cross stitch sampler spotted at an antique show. Designed by Beverly Conway. Hooked by Davey DeGraff. Vermont. 1996. 28" x 56". *Courtesy of Davey DeGraff.*

Buffy, the Maltese poodle, waits for her owners to return. Her tiny face can very faintly be seen in the side window on the lower right side. Fanciful birds and animals gather around "Buffy's House," including a large plaid cat on the roof. Adapted from "Farwood." Lib Callaway pattern / Hook Nook. Hooked by Elizabeth Morgan. Vermont. 2000. 20.5" x 36". *Courtesy of Elizabeth Morgan.*

"Pumpkin House." The former Massachusetts home of American folk art collectors, Bertram and Nina Little. Designed by Edyth O'Neill. Woolley Fox pattern. Hooked by Eloise Murray. Texas. 2004. 13" x 14". *Courtesy of Eloise Murray.*

Window boxes and a kitty on the front step welcome you "Home." Designed and hooked by Debbie Torre. Rhode Island. 2002. 8' x 3'. *Courtesy of Debbie Torre*.

"Fogg Farm." "This rug is the story of the first time my father saw my mother. My father, Cecil Wentworth, was attending the University of New Hampshire in Durham in 1927. He and a friend were going out of town in his yellow Stutz Bearcat convertible and had to take a detour that brought them to the corner where my mother, Emily Fogg, lived. She was at the mailbox and he made a comment like, 'There's a good looking girl going to waste out in the country.' He met her later that year." Adapted from an old photograph. Made into a pattern by Betsy Burton. Hooked by Lee Abrego. New Hampshire. 2005. 31" x 45". *Courtesy of Lee Abrego.*

No home is complete without a dog, cats, and a white picket fence. "My Farmhouse." Designed and hooked by Pam Evans. Rhode Island. 1999. 29.5" x 33.5". *Courtesy of Pam Evans.*

"The Weare Homestead." "My great grandparents' home in York, Maine, where I spent summers as a child. Lots of fond memories..." Designed and hooked by Deb Foster. Maine. 2002. 18" x 24". *Courtesy of Deb Foster.*

The Colors of Jan Winter—Hollywood, California

There is no denying Jan Winter's love for color. It dominates her hooked work and creates an upbeat atmosphere. A longtime quilter, Jan picked up a hook in 1992 and hasn't looked back. The following pages clearly illustrate this award winning artist's vibrant personality and talent.

A sea of fanciful anemones with firework-like bursts of color. Choosing a rich dark background not only intensifies the color, it helps create a sense of depth. "Flamboyancy." Designed by Mildred Sprout. Hooked by Jan Winter. California. 2002. 60" x 36". *Courtesy of Jan Winter.*

Finely shaded oak leaf clusters join decorative corner motifs to form an ornate border around a simple striped basket weave pattern. The fluid curving outer lines are in sharp contrast to the angular center, creating a visually striking composition. "Eastham Moors." Lib Callaway pattern / Hook Nook. Hooked by Jan Winter. California. 72" x 48". *Courtesy of Jan Winter.*

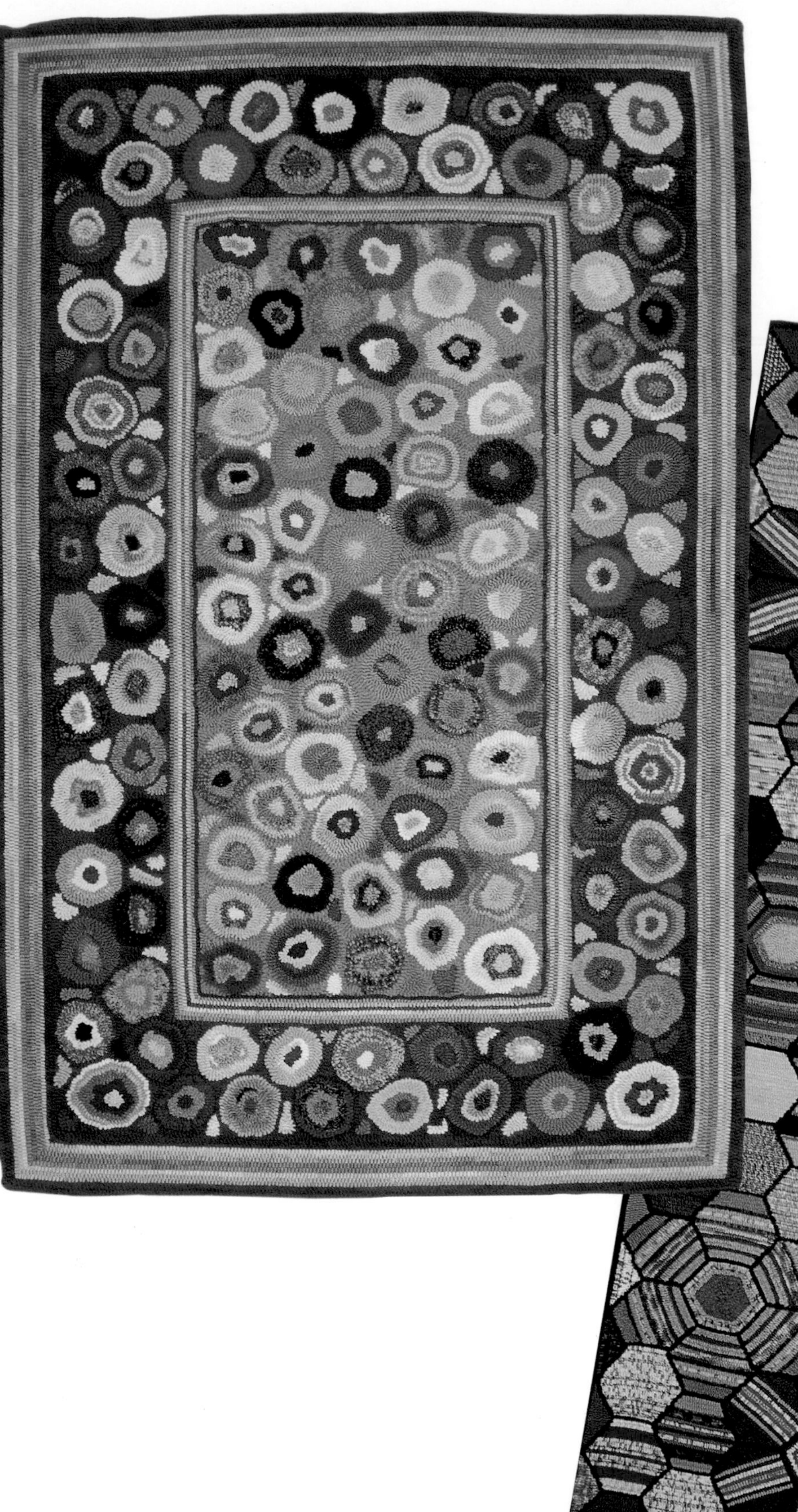

Concentric borders contain "Mille Fleur." Designed by Jane McGown Flynn. House of Price / Charco pattern. Hooked by Jan Winter. California. 1997. 50" x 31". *Courtesy of Jan Winter.*

"Stars and Stripes." Hexagons gone wild. Designed and hooked by Jan Winter. California. 2003. 83" x 35". *Courtesy of Jan Winter.*

A polychrome display of stylized saw-toothed diamonds. "Stepping Stones." Designed and hooked by Jan Winter. California. 1995. 85" x 39". *Courtesy of Jan Winter.*

A watercolor impression of "Prudence." Designed by Pearl McGown. W. Cushing and Company pattern. Hooked by Jan Winter. California. 2000. 71" x 39". *Courtesy of Jan Winter.*

Suggested Reading

Beatty, Alice, and Mary Sargent. *Basic Rug Hooking*. Harrisburg, Pennsylvania: Stackpole Books, 1990.

Boswell, Thom, ed. *The Rug Hook Book: Techniques, Projects and Patterns for This Easy Traditional Craft*. New York: Sterling Publishing Co. Inc., 1992.

Burton, Mary Sheppard. *A Passion for the Creative Life: Textiles to Lift the Spirit*. Edited by Mary Ellen Cooper. Germantown, Maryland: Sign of the Hook Books, 2002.

Carroll, Barbara. *American Folk Art Rug Hooking—18 Folk Art Projects with Rug Hooking Basics, Tips & Techniques*. Urbandale, Iowa: Landauer Books, 2005.

Davies, Ann. *Rag Rugs: How to Use Ancient and Modern Rug-Making Techniques to Create Rugs, Wallhangings, Even Jewelry—12 Projects*. New York: Henry Holt and Company, Inc., 1992.

Field, Jeanne. *Shading Flowers: The Complete Guide for Rug Hookers*. Harrisburg, Pennsylvania: Stackpole Books, 1991.

Kent, William, W. *The Hooked Rug*. New York: Tudor Publishing Company, 1930.

Kent, William W. *Hooked Rug Design*. Springfield, Massachusetts: Pond-Ekberg Company, 1949.

Kent, William W. *Rare Hooked Rugs*. Springfield, Massachusetts: The Pond-Ekberg Company, 1941.

Kopp, Joel and Kate. *American Hooked and Sewn Rugs: Folk Art Underfoot*. New York: E.P. Dutton, Inc., 1975.

Lais, Emma Lou, and Barbara Carroll. *American Primitive Hooked Rugs: Primer for Re-Creating Antique Rugs*. Kennebunkport, Maine: Wildwood Press, 1999.

Linsey, Leslie. *Hooked Rugs: An American Folk Art*. New York, New York: Clarkson N. Potter. Inc., 1992.

Logsdon, Roslyn. *People and Places: Roslyn Logsdon's Imagery in Fiber*. Rug Hooking Magazine's Framework Series Edition. Harrisburg, Pennsylvania: David Detweiler, 1998.

Mather, Anne D. *Creative Rug Hooking*. New York, New York: Sterling Company, 2000.

McGown, Pearl K. *Color In Hooked Rugs*. Boston: Buck Printing Co., 1954.

McGown, Pearl K. *Dreams Beneath the Designs*. Boston: Bruce Humphries Inc., 1939.

McGown, Pearl K. *The Lore and Lure of Hooked Rugs*. Acton, Massachusetts: Acton Press, 1966.

McGown, Pearl K. *You ...Can Hook Rugs*. Boston: Buck Printing Co., 1951.

Minick, Polly, and Laurie Simpson. *Folk Art Friends: Hooked Rugs and Coordinating Quilts*. Woodinville, Washington: Martingale and Company, 2003.

Moshimer, Joan. *Hooked on Cats: Complete Patterns and Instructions for Rug Hookers*. Harrisburg, Pennsylvania: Stackpole Books, 1991.

Moshimer, Joan. *The Complete Rug Hooker.* Boston: New York Graphic Society, 1975.

Oxford, Amy. *Hooked Rugs Today*. Atglen, Pennsylvania: Schiffer Publishing Ltd., 2005.

Oxford, Amy. *Punch Needle Rug Hooking: Techniques and Designs*. Atglen, Pennsylvania: Schiffer Publishing Ltd., 2003.

Peladeau, Mildred C. *Art Underfoot: The Story of the Waldoboro Hooked Rugs*. Lowell, Massachusetts: American Textile History Museum, 1999.

Siano, Margaret, and Susan Huxley. *The Secrets of Finishing Hooked Rugs*. Lemoyne, Pennsylvania: Rug Hooking Magazine, 2003.

Tennant, Emma. *Rag Rugs of England and America*. London, England: Walker Books, 1992.

Thompson, Nancy Butts. *Hooking on the Hill*. Georgia: Nancy Butts Thompson, 2005.

Turbayne, Jessie A. *Hooked Rugs: History and the Continuing Tradition.* West Chester, Pennsylvania: Schiffer Publishing Ltd., 1991.

Turbayne, Jessie A. *Hooked Rug Treasury.* Atglen, Pennsylvania: Schiffer Publishing Ltd., 1997.

Turbayne, Jessie A. *The Big Book of Hooked Rugs 1950–1980s*. Atglen, Pennsylvania: Schiffer Publishing Ltd., 2005.

Turbayne, Jessie A. *The Complete Guide to Collecting Hooked Rugs: Unrolling the Secrets*. Atglen, Pennsylvania: Schiffer Publishing Ltd., 2004.

Turbayne, Jessie A. *The Hooker's Art*. Atglen, Pennsylvania: Schiffer Publishing Ltd., 1993.

Yoder, Patty. *The Alphabet of Sheep.* Raleigh, North Carolina: Ivy House Publishing Group, 2003.

Young, Arthur. *America Gets Hooked: History of a Folk Art*. Lewiston Maine: Booksplus, 1994.